MW00586188

Jesus and Mary Magdalene:

The Eternal Heart of Love

Volume One

As revealed by Jeshua
through Yael and Doug Powell

Circle of Light Press
Eureka Springs, Arkansas
2009

Jesus and Mary Magdalene:
The Eternal Heart of Love
Volume One
As revealed by Jeshua
through Yael and Doug Powell

Copyright 2009 by Yael and Doug Powell
Circle of Light Press
3969 Mundell Road
Eureka Springs, AR 72631

Paperback Original ISBN 0-9725991-7-7
978-0-9725991-7-7

Cover Art by Willa Davidsohn
Excerpts (with permission) from poetry by Naomi Stone
Book design, layout by Judith Bicking
Editing by Shanna Mac Lean
Printing by InstantPublisher.com Collierville, TN

Websites: www.circleoflight.net and www.unitingtwinflames.com
Email: connect@circleoflight.net
Telephone: 479-253-6832, 479-253-2774

FROM CIRCLE OF LIGHT PRESS

On Jesus and Mary Magdalene

Jesus and Mary Magdalene:
The Eternal Heart of Love,
Volume I

Jesus and Mary Magdalene:
Creating the Pattern of Light for Earth,
Volume II
To be released soon

On SoulMates (Twin Flames)

Say "Yes" to Love, God Explains SoulMates

Say "Yes" to Love, God Unveils SoulMate Love
and Sacred Sexuality

Eternal Twin Flame Love, The Story of ShannaPra
By Shanna Mac Lean

On Christ Consciousness

Say "Yes" to Love, God Leads Humanity Toward
Christ Consciousness

Say "Yes" to Love, Giving Birth to a World of Love

On Animal Communication

Say "Yes" to Love, Magic Cat (an enlightened
animal) Explains Creation

DEDICATION

I dedicate this book to my beautiful husband, Doug, my own Twin Flame, who IS my heart and whose Love is my pathway to freedom. You are amazing!

I dedicate this book also to humanity, my beautiful brothers and sisters, with whom I am here to share, to love and to serve.

And, I dedicate this book to God, The Beloved, that infinite Love and boundless Life beyond imagining, in gratitude for the intimate and mystical Communion that has blessed, sustained and grown me and opened me to Jeshua and Mary.

ACKNOWLEDGEMENTS

Heartfelt thanks to Willa Davidsohn, my mother and a fabulous artist, for the wonderful cover art. Willa, you captured Mary Magdalene right away and I am so grateful. You gave of yourself, your time and your amazing talent so generously and lovingly. I'm so honored to have your work grace our covers and to have you as my mother. You are an exceptional woman.

I'd like to express my deepest gratitude to Naomi Stone for the gift of her amazing poetry. It expresses so perfectly the awakening of the heart and the mystery of the Spirit as it moves us. I feel honored to have excerpts from Naomi's poetry grace these pages. To Naomi, these inspired words are simply her recording of the movement of that Great Love within her. By whatever definition, her words are markers of a great wonder that is very difficult to describe. She does this brilliantly. Thank you, Naomi.

I would like to give special and heartfelt thanks to Shanna Mac Lean, spirit sister, dearest friend and tireless worker for the Light. Without you, Shanna, our books would not exist. Thank you for all the endless hours of typing, editing, and your skillful organization of all that flows through Circle of Light. And most of all, thank you for your support, your dedication to this work, your Love and your deep devotion to God. I am continually grateful for – and amazed by – you!

AN INTRODUCTION FOR THE READER
by Yael Powell

I was raised in a Jewish household with no exposure to Jesus. In fact, my father was not neutral, but against any discussion that included Jesus' name in any way at all. So I had no preconceived ideas about who Jeshua is.

My first experience with him came as a complete surprise. I was standing in a field in Louisiana in 1969. I was 19 years old and I was at my first music festival. It was one of those moments where, although surrounded with people, I felt completely and utterly alone. I raised my eyes. The sky became luminous, like a galaxy filled with whirling Light and stars, and in an instant everything opened and I saw The Plan. I saw the Brotherhood and Sisterhood of Light and I saw Jeshua, the one we know as Jesus. He touched my heart like an arrow of Love and brought forth in me a powerful feeling of devotion to his cause that has never left me.

I went to that festival as a party girl, and I left as a flower child, dedicated to creating a world of Love and peace. Then, in 1983, I was desperate, in intractable pain, having just received a diagnosis of a hereditary illness that had been stalking me. In an agony of emotion and body, I cried out for help and told God that I didn't want to live like this and needed help or I would take my own life.

The next morning as I sat to meditate — something I had been doing daily since my early experiences — I was lifted into a communion of Love so intimate, so deep, so tender and yet so filled with Light and so vast that it changed my life. It gave me strength and gave me the courage to live. That communion with God was the beginning of a life dedicated to awakening this Love and bringing the gift of this communion with God to everyone, knowing that it is ours. It is for all of us.

Periodically Jeshua (Jesus) would come to me over the years, and my relationship with him deepened and evolved. Yet for me, the center of my life and my spiritual practice was the communion with our Creator. Then a number of years ago, as I sat in meditation, God (Goddess, Creator – whatever word you would like to use since it is beyond words, anyway) lifted me into an experience of shared consciousness with Jesus as he went through the last hours of his life on Earth and experienced what we know as the Resurrection.

As with so many things that I have been shown, this powerful experience completely turned me around, shook me, opened me and left me seeing things very differently. I believe that was the moment this book began, although I didn't know it. I experienced in full measure the amazing heart that is the heart of Christ that lived on Earth as Jesus/Jeshua.

In another communion with Jesus that was part of a workshop given here at Circle of Light, Jeshua came to me and delivered a gift of the Transforming Heart that I now share with my beloved Twin Flame, my husband Doug. It is a connection to the vortex of Love, the transforming power of grace that is anchored on Earth by Jeshua and his Twin Flame, Mary Magdalene. This Transforming Heart was connected to our heart and I was asked to use it to assist people to transform old heart's beliefs that were keeping them from being free and from being true and open conduits for Love. As I began working with people in this capacity, using this Transforming Heart, Jeshua would come to assist me in every session. My relationship with him deepened and he became more and more "real" to me, more a part of my daily life. I became more familiar with his energy and with how he appeared in the realms of Light.

He then came to me in meditation one day last September, and showed me his Love with Mary, the Magdalene. He asked me if I would be willing to write about this for him, to be the conduit, to share this important information with humankind. He said, "It is time." Of course, I said, "yes." Thus, this book began.

It has truly been an amazing experience, very different from my experiences with God in meditation. Every communion with Jeshua is so clear and in such living color, it is like being with him through those times. For me it has been a gift in so many unexpected ways, including the experience of the gift of travel (in Volume II). I have been physically unable to travel at all for probably thirty years and for twenty of those years I was almost completely housebound. While I have been given the great gift of communion in the realms of Light, this experience of traveling the world, seeing it through the eyes of Jeshua and his beloved, Mary, has been incredible.

When I open to him, Jesus appears to me as if he were physical but made out of luminous particles of dancing Light. As this work has progressed, he often simply appears spontaneously, for example, when I open my eyes from sleep. At these times, his form is completely recognizable and his presence is palpable and real. He is beyond handsome. And yet, he glows and he is vibrant. I can feel the Light and see it pouring from him.

When I see Jeshua standing before me, what I see is not the thin, sallow being we have so often seen portrayed. Rather, I see a gloriously masculine man, breathtakingly beautiful, alive and radiant in his Love. I know that this is how he appeared on Earth as well – perfect in every way. He is the perfection of God made manifest, the tangible expression of God's Love, appearing in human form. He IS the Divine Masculine. He never ceases to amaze me.

When Mary Magdalene first came to me, I had the same experience of recognition and the deep knowledge in my heart that she too was the perfect expression of the Creator as feminine. She was vibrant, beautiful, filled with life, exuberant and full of delight and humor, expressing a pure and glorious Love in a form that we know as woman.

When they appear, it is as if they are standing with me in the room, although I am aware that they are not solid. It doesn't matter if my eyes are open or closed. They are still there. And yet, they are made of Light. Each one is recognizable to me instantly by his/her energy, just as you would know one of your best friends by how they "feel." The combination of the feeling, the appearance, the energy, the Light, the electricity and the movement of spirit and Love make it irrefutable to my heart that I am in the presence of the Creator's heart expressed as the Twin Flame heart of pure Love that is Jesus and Mary Magdalene.

Then, they begin to share their story with me. It is instantly clear who is speaking by who stands to the front and comes in the most clearly and whose voice I hear. I just speak into my recorder what I see as they show me and guide me through the unfolding scenes of their life on Earth. This is how this book has come to be, as well as the other books that are in process in the series (stay tuned!).

I am humbly grateful beyond the capacity of any words to express for the honor of serving with my beloved husband, Doug, as the conduit for their story, for their Love and for the balanced energy of the Divine Masculine and Divine Feminine that they brought to Earth. This is what they are activating with us now. It is one of the main purposes of these books. The time is here for all of us to release the old identities that we have acquired as limited humans and to step into our truth as the Creator's Love, as the Divine Masculine or the Divine Feminine. It is the moment to become aware of our Twin Flame counterpart and know that the Christ coming again, as us, will be balanced, and Earth life will be restored to the truth of only Love.

I looked out upon the rolling hills and saw the sheep dotting the hillside and a shepherd boy tending them. In my heart I knew that God, the living and endless Love, is ever that which shepherds us. I saw humanity as those sheep grazing, needing care. In my heart, I said, "Beloved Creator, I will be their shepherd in Your name, as Your Love, always." So was this analogy born. I am as the shepherd. Human hearts are what He/She tends. As I open as that living spirit, then I am one with the living God of Love and I am the shepherd of humanity.

So I was. And so I am, here to guide you, every one of you, as the Creator lives and breathes and loves, loves you as me, and loves me through you and the great circle of Love continues.

Jeshua ben Joseph

The beloved mystery grants
a union of hearts
far beyond the reach
of the world
to those who
give all for love.

Chapter One

"I came as a fiery comet..."

Jeshua speaks:

I am the one whom you know as Jeshua or Jesus. I come to you to share with you the story of my life on Earth and of my Love with my beloved Mary who was also known as the Magdalene. Most of all, I have come at this time to turn the key and open your remembrance of all the beauty, the tenderness and the power of the Creator's Love as it lives in you and you live in it.

To some of you, the things I share you will already know. To others, they may seem fantastic. But in the turning of this Age and the opening of the world to a greater Love, it is time for the remembrance of who you are. That is why I come — to share with you the story of my life that you might place your focus on the truth for you and remember that all that I am, you are also.

As I lived, so shall you — without limits, every door opening to you instantly, basking in the Creator's Love, living in wonder in a land of beauty, in a world of peace, functioning as the Light you are, grounded in God's Love. Where you choose to place your focus is what you accord, and what you accord, you shall create. I use the word "accord" purposefully because in this language no other word will do. It means to agree to something in harmony with others and in a harmony that produces results.

You are the power of the Creator's focus brought forth into the world, so what you accord is of great importance, especially at this time. As the Creator's Love lives and has Its being in you, it is brought forth through your heart into the world that you might live this Love as your life. It is my prayer that you live in joy, dancing with the mystery.

When I came to Earth, I came as a fiery comet, dropping from the Heavens into the world with all my spiritual Light still blazing. My abilities to see were wide awake because I came into the world through a new agreement, the entry of pure Love into the illusion of life on Earth. I came to parents who brought me from the living realms of God down the vibrational scale consciously and into the world, pulling the atoms that would create my body to them and giving me the gift of pure Light that was never interrupted.

I grew up a happy child, helping Joseph in his workshop and Mary with her chores. Through their patience, persistence and beautiful efforts, their purity and their Love, I was introduced to the deeper teachings and rituals of worship that they shared. I learned the esoteric wisdom and the ways of holding great patterns of Light for the Earth — keeping my heart pure and open to be able to be that experience of God, the living Christ, the open heart, in full remembrance of who and what it is. I cannot do justice to their glory and to all that they held for God in the world. Their Love for humanity was true and unwavering and nothing was more important to them than holding the pure vibration of God's Love and preparing the vehicle I am for humanity as perfectly as they could.

In telling my story and my Love with Mary Magdalene, I give you a true picture of Real Love and what it means to be a Twin Flame heart, eternally. - Twin Flames are always worshiping the One, dancing through every moment of life in ecstasy and the joy of expressing Love for God. We are ever and always giving forth that which we so generously receive from our beloved Creator every moment. The Love is amplified through the ecstasy of our own Twin Flame heart and then poured forth, again and again, forever.

As we enter this time of awakening and each of you feels the Twin Flame rising in your own heart, please remember that it is not another's energy outside of you that is calling you. It is part of your very own life stream. You are one Love with two streams of consciousness that rise and dance in worship. Two energies are in motion, and without the two energies there would be no creation, only stillness. While stillness is beautiful and necessary as a background, there is no energy generated, no force or spark of creation, no life exploding forth in all its splendor.

What makes the great life that is God manifest as spiritual truth is the continual movement of Divine Masculine and Divine Feminine coming together and moving apart. It is truly that which drives Creation. It is the unlimited energy source that powers the expression of the living hologram of Love that God is.

So I share with you the glory of my Love for God and the indescribable beauty of my Love with Mary, my beloved. I share with you the way we lived and moved and perceived the world, working in accord with All That Is, alive to the living hum that is The Word — letting it live and move and have its being in us and delighting in that spark, that Light, that joy of infinity as it showed itself to us in every life.

We lived always in the understanding that we are Light. We are energy and Love in unison. We are the coming together of that Light of the Masculine and the great eternal Love of the Divine as Feminine, as they bring forth the mystery of Creation.

To you it might seem magical that we lived in a world truly without barriers and that the spirit spoke to us and through us. But it is true. We were in continual and open communication with every being who would accord us.

It is also true for you. You are here to open these doors of remembrance now for the world. Thus, I bring our story and within it the voice of the Angels, the movement of the breath of the Creator and the codes of Light and Love that will become, for you, that deep remembrance.

Of course, you and I know each other and have eternally. I am the Light of the living Christos and of course, so are you — as Mary is the great ever-moving and pulsing Love of the glorious Divine Feminine.

Please assist me as I endeavor to place these experiences in words that can somehow encompass them, especially beyond the limitations of gender. The Divine as Masculine and the Divine as Feminine are so far beyond what human life perceives. It is truly the movement of Creation in its embodiment as consciousness, as energy, as Love and as you.

Come with delight and share this story with us — with me and with my beloved Mary, the Magdalene. Let me paint for you the picture of how we lived and loved and how we served this very awakening, knowing always that we came for you who are living in this time.

Mary Magdalene speaks:

I am the one called Mary. I am the Magdalene, which was an office of honor. I was an initiate in the Temple of Women, the Temple of the Goddess, the Temple dedicated to the great Divine Feminine in all Her expressions in all Creation.

I understood before I came into the world that I would be vilified. I knew that the time was coming when human power would have more appeal than the power of God/Goddess. The swing of the pendulum of the world would move to the masculine and I would be called a harlot or a prostitute. But I was no more a prostitute than you are, any of you, even those who might have dreamed it for a while.

We are all children of the living God/Goddess and we are one song of Love. Yes, I was trained in the way of Divine Love Making but this is far different from the current picture of sexuality. It is Love-Making that is totally focused on the pinnacle of Light and the power of the great pulsations of Creation. It is the acknowledgement that those energies are born in us and live through us to make manifest all that we dream and all that we love.

We did celebrate the rituals of this highest Love in the Goddess Temple. I accorded it with all the others

5

and helped to bring this energy into the world in dedication to the living Goddess/God. I was trained in the highest forms of true Love Making and this is what I brought to my beloved Jeshua, showing him many things of which he was not aware, since his focus was firmly on the pure Light and not on the world.

I showed him the ocean of Love that is the feminine and how it is meant to be the grounding of our being, and I showed him that the Light and power of the masculine is our impetus to create. We truly are the embodiment of the movement of Creation, that which in the Temple we called the Dance of the Goddess and God. We knew that those expressions were simply ways to describe something that is ever unspeakable.

I was not one who participated in those rituals, nor was I a priestess who initiated men. Had I been, I would have done so with joy, knowing it as the greatest honor. I remind you, of course, what you already know — that every expression of sexuality exists in the world. The fear of the Divine Feminine became so all encompassing to the ones who sought power — power over others, not the power of God — that they had to vilify the feminine, because in Her the world is brought to wholeness. It is impossible in Her Love to have power over another.

All the power of true Love-Making had to be dismantled and the deep abiding wisdom of the Goddess eradicated, if, in those times of men, those who sought power over others were to gain their objective. Thus, they made me the harlot. But I understood before I came that this would happen. I also saw the patterns, the swing of the energies that would come back, first, all the way to the other side to be the reaction of women to the misogamy of men. Then with the turning of the Age, life on Earth would return to the center and to the true understanding of Real Love and how it is embodied as Twin Flames such as Jeshua and me.

And so I danced the dance of life on Earth in joy and wonder and I always felt the Creator's Love. I laughed and played and gloried in the wonder of Nature and delighted in the beauty of the body. All of it was one singing harmony that was ever a Love Song to God/Goddess, a song in which we are the notes and we are the changes in the chords. We are the expression of that holographic Love wherever we focus.

I hope that you will feel me in this story and that you will get a sense of my delight in life and how I came to truly be the incarnation of the Creator's Love, the Divine Feminine, the Goddess. Everything I did, I did for this. My Love for Jeshua is greater than the limited form, greater than the heart of Mary, the Magdalene. My Love for Jeshua is as eternal as the Love of God, and as powerful.

I knew in my heart and spirit this Love of ours from the moment I first was born, for I always had a perspective open to the etheric realm and I always knew the Love of my Twin. I felt and knew him before I met him in the physical, and even then, I always saw what he truly was. I saw the patterns of Light. I saw our life together, and I saw the sacrifice.

It is my hope that in this story you will reclaim your delight, your joy, your wonder at life — that the energy of the Creator can find a home in you and that you can reclaim your true sacred sexuality and use it to open the gateway to the New World that we are now ushering in.

I see all of you clearly from the realms of spirit and every one of you is my dearest and most delightful friend. I invite each one of you to make the connection with me and to find out who I am, firsthand, for I promise to come to you in your time of silence, of meditation. All you have to do is ask me.

As you read these pages and as Jeshua and I share the story of our Love, its eternal nature and our awareness of our mission, I hope that you will feel me and that you will join me in my laughter and join me in my Love for Jeshua who truly is a miracle. He is the voice of God on Earth and he is still here as that living Christos, that connection of pure Love with you. I am ever here as the Love of the Divine Feminine to bring him to you and to assist in every way I can to anchor his Love in the world.

May the spaces between us
always be blessed
and so filled with
the Beloved,
there will be no distance between
our hearts and souls.

Chapter Two

"As children, Mary and I danced and played upon the hills..."

Jeshua speaks:

I come to tell the story of my Love with Mary Magdalene because it is time to bring this awareness to the world. It is time for the awakening of the knowledge of Twin Flames. All that has been separate in Creation must be made whole again and that which has seen itself as masculine and feminine must come together in the center to be a wholeness and to remember the truth of the one heart of God.

I begin with my birth for there are things that are important for you to know. Though I was born through the body of a woman, I did not come into the world in the normal way. I came to Earth free of the ego dream in which you live, free of the ego's overlay, free of the identities of the human mind.

I came to be the living Arc of the Covenant of God with His/Her people. My mission was to bring the highest Light of Our Beloved Creator all the way deeply into the world that the world might remember its divine unity — remember the song in which every life appearing here remembers its part and joins with all others in divine harmony.

My birth was the birth of God's purity into the mortal world of human beings. It happened by the Will of Love and unity through two magnificent and divinely guided people. Joseph was a priest of the highest order in the Mystery Schools that kept the true flame of God burning for the world. Mary, my mother, as you already know, is a glorious being. She came into Earth life without ever forgetting who she is and what she had promised to do for God.

Together my Earthly father and mother harnessed the divine energies of their spirits, embodying the living flame of Twin Flame Love. By their Will, they used The Word, the living OM, to bring this Light I hold for God, for the One, down into this world. They implanted it directly in Mary's womb and nurtured it, using holy breath and the living voice that is the embodiment of the spirit of God for the world.

Mary and Joseph nourished this Light, drawing to it conscious cells to create a body untainted by duality, the body of an infant made of atoms still resonating with the highest Light that coalesced at their call. I waited for their call and through my Love for the Creator, I came and joined myself with Mary at the moment of birth to bring the living Christ into the world.

I never knew the anguish of being human and never saw the darkness in the world. Instead I lived and played, as do most children, in a paradise of unity and joy as I danced through the fields of Nature and spoke with the flowers. All around me were ever the cosmic Lights that merged in a glorious field of Oneness that appeared to physical eyes as the Earth. But the Earth I lived in was made of living spirit, and the atoms danced to the eternal tune of Love. The voices of the Nature

Spirits spoke to me, and all of us rejoiced in God and in our Love for Him/Her.

I grew up knowing in my heart my mission and recognizing there were many spokes in the wheel, many things that I had to join together through my heart to unite all people with the Covenant of God's remembrance. This is why I traveled. Not to study, although I did, but so that I might be versed in the teachings of the various paths to spirit. Mostly I traveled to make my connections with people who would remember their part in the drama being brought to birth. Through me, everyone could remember their true Love and recognize their place in the whole.

I went to India, to Persia, to Egypt, to all the places where the Light burns brightly and I met with priests and priestesses and magicians. I met with those who lived in the Himalayas who held the song of God as living Masters and we knew each other instantly and deeply. All acknowledged the remembrance of this teaching that was my life.

I walked the world in beauty and in trust, constantly in communion with the true Beloved, Our Creator, and all things were shown to me easily and instantly. I knew intimately the glorious song of life. I sang it, merging the world and the spirit through my body and offering myself as the living bridge in order to re-establish the connection between God and humankind.

In my early years I traveled with Mary and Joseph (I always saw God as my true Mother and Father, and Mary and Joseph as my divine guardians). As I grew, I traveled on my own, my safekeeping entrusted to those men and women who formed the vast network of Light of which Joseph and Mary were part. Although I did spend time with my family in Nazareth and did learn Joseph's trade, it was never the focus. Mary and Joseph knew who I am, and my formative years were completely dedicated to my mission.

When I emerged from my travels I met my beloved, Mary Magdalene. It was not that I didn't know her, because, oh, I did, but we had different paths of preparation for our work. She was being prepared to be the full embodiment of the Divine Feminine. She studied with the priestesses in the Goddess School that she might learn to be this burning cauldron of Love that would ignite in me the remembrance of our Twin Flame union and all that we could be on Earth for God.

That blazing Light that was our unified heart had its beginning in her, because I was so focused on bringing in God's Covenant that my focus was on humanity completely. I paid little attention to myself or even to my masculinity because the body to me was just an extension of the living spirit. I saw the atoms dancing and I communed with them, and I knew that I looked to others the same as they did. But I knew my body simply as the Light that allowed my grand and glorious spirit to focus here in the world to serve.

But Mary, being brought up in the Goddess School, was taught the ways of sacred Love and she was taught how to ignite this Love through the physical, that it might become the Arc of the Covenant from here. So rather than bringing the spirit into the world as I did, her work was to bring the remembrance of spirit from the things of the world back Home. Her training was about true Love, and the union of the body and the flame of Love that burns as sexuality that is part of the constant movement of Creation. I always felt this and knew it within my heart but I hadn't experienced it here on Earth through the physical.

Mary and I knew each other as children. In truth, I fell in Love with Mary when we were five and six years old. I knew even then that she was my heart. We knew the purity of Love as it was meant to be, as young children often do. We danced and played upon the hills and romped with the sheep and goats, and it felt to us as if all the world responded to our requests. Truly the flowers danced for us and the sun sang our names. We felt the warmth of the Creator's Love and knew it as ourselves.

We would go out in the mornings, packing our lunch of barley cakes that we ate with goat cheese and olives. Carrying a basket between us we would head for the hills where we would sit and laugh and sing. I would hold her hand and she would kiss my cheek. I would look at her with such Love, and we knew that we were together the song of the Creator's Love, being prepared to be sung for the Earth.

We would find a place where the scrub grass didn't grow, and taking a stick we would draw in the sandy soil the great signs and movements of the Heavens and the turning of the Ages. We would speak about what I was to bring to the Age in which we lived, and how she was bringing the energies for the next Age.

We came in carrying the perfect Light and didn't come all the way into the world but lived above the sub-creation that the ego built, so we could always see true Love. Both of us looked different in our appearance than the tribe within which we were born, most of whom had dark hair, dark eyes, and very distinct facial features.

I, carrying the white Light of Divine Masculine woven into the expression of that body, did appear as blonde and blue-eyed, as close to the Light as a human could express. Mary, always the representative of the Divine Feminine and even then holding a Queen's countenance, carried the gold of Divine Feminine and expressed it physically in beautiful hair of red/gold that shone like fire and sunlight and eyes that were golden green, pure gold in the sun. She had a smile that could melt your heart.

Our parents understood what was meant for us and so allowed us, as children, our solitude together and helped to prepare us for the Twin Flame Love that we were embodying for the world. But our time together was meant to be short lived, and both of us knew it. We felt it. So we cherished our times together, our afternoons with the goats and our long conversations with the shepherds.

When I was seven I was taken away to live in the community of the Essenes at Mt. Hermon. Mary began being prepared for the Temple of the mysteries of women. But we always saw each other in the spirit because those doorways were ever open to us. At night when I would lay on my cot, I would commune with her and share what I was learning. She would share with me. Later we found when we came together again that the knowledge had indeed transferred, and she knew many things that I had been taught that had not been given to her, and vice versa.

In the community of the Essenes I learned how to integrate all the things I was aware of in God, with the human lives I was here to serve. I went through many initiations, most of which were deeply secret and I had many wonderful mentors who sensed, if not knew, what I was on Earth to bring. But I was never treated any differently from any other boy. As I grew into a young man I began to learn of co-creatorhood and what it meant to be the "son of God."

All this time I had my Mary's Love. My Twin Flame heart was alive and burning. Mostly at night, because of my busy days, we put our flames together. As I grew toward puberty, though the pull of the body was not that strong, I felt the awakening of something within my heart that named itself my beloved Mary. We began to experience the dance of Love in a new way, aligned with the Creator, another level of ecstasy and a deeper experience of worship as we loved God as one.

Then, when I was seventeen, the time came for me to travel. I insisted on seeing Mary again but it wasn't to be allowed. I left and went to India and to Egypt and studied, again connecting the lines of wisdom and energy that were present in the world with the truth of God and the weaving of a new Age that I was anchoring.

In this time my nights became infused with a Light brighter than even I had experienced to this point. I knew it was my soul, my spirit, my heart in conjunction with Mary's, weaving together in a unity of pure Love of God. Yet it was a flame that also burned on every level and I was assisted with the things that I was learning in making sure this energy was raised to the highest vibration and that our union was in alignment with what is Real.

I spoke to the man who had trained me who had become a wonderful mentor. As we were sitting in his cave together, he explained to me the power of our Love and what it meant to carry these flames into the world. He revealed how he saw our stars woven together, mine and Mary's, who would be called the Magdalene. My heart leaped in joy because I had confirmation of what I had felt, and I couldn't wait to see my beloved Mary again. I waited truly with baited breath for the time that I could leave.

I knew also that it was important that I made these connections and wove together the teachings of the world into a new teaching or experience of eternal Love that would usher in the coming Ages and the world's transformation. So I continued to study and dialog and build these bridges with the wise ones and learn how to master every level, including the level of the physical.

All the while I heard my beloved singing her Love song into my soul. I would rise up declaring my endless Love and we would worship God together. It was beautiful beyond every dream and all description.

*Oh, beautiful light of my life,
inspiration of my soul
and the one who opens my heart!
I awaken in this silent darkness
and feel the ever-expanding joy
your presence gives.*

Chapter Three

"I was here to worship at her feet..."

The time came for me to return home and to be in Jerusalem for the high Holy Days. I couldn't wait to see my Mary and to feel her radiant Love. We actually sent messages to each other on the physical level and arranged a place to meet on a certain street that was quiet, as streets go, in Jerusalem. We set a date and a time.

When I came into Jerusalem on caravan, the first thing I wanted to do was run to that street but I made myself stop and go to the Holy Temple of the Jews, taking time to wash the dust off of my feet. I wanted to present myself to the Rabbis there as a teacher, to express to them what I desired to teach and to worship God at the holy altar there, once again honoring all paths to the awakening of Love and the awareness of God in the world.

At last it was time and I left the Temple, walking carefully down the street, suddenly feeling anxious, having butterflies in my stomach, knowing it was my true Love I went to meet. Having no experience in the physical with interacting with the opposite sex, I had some moments of feeling nervous, not apprehensive, but just hesitant, afraid I wouldn't know what to do.

She was standing there in the middle of the dusty street. Her hair was a golden-red halo flaming out all around her. Her fire was so bright it was like a thousand suns. What I saw of her beautiful heart filled me with such awe and reverence that my cheeks were full of tears. Mary had always been recognized as special and everyone acknowledged that she carried a great Light, but that Light had burst free of all of its confines and she was radiant beyond all description.

I was speechless. I fell totally head over heels in Love. She smiled at me, that smile of hers that was so beautiful and so mysterious where just the corners of her mouth turned upward. All I could think was how I longed to join with her and to let the flame of Love consume us until we became the living song of worship of God. She knew every thought I had. She felt every feeling in my heart and I swear, she even knew the rate of my heart beat as it beat so fast I could hardly breathe.

I had returned from my travels believing that I was worldly and knowledgeable and that I had accomplished many important things, including the conquering of the energies of the body — as if I were living as a normal human. But in that moment when I saw Mary, radiant in her womanhood, standing in the sunlight on the street, I knew that all that I had learned was as nothing, and that I was here to worship at her feet and to learn the song of life from her — she who held the other part of my being.

Then I heard the voice of God within me. It spoke and said, "She is the one, the other half of your own being, and I, God, sanctify this Love." I fell to my knees in that street and tears rolled down my face and I breathed, "Thank You, God," with every breath. When I raised my eyes she was looking at me, and our souls leaped from the confines of the body and joined right there as we were, in the street. Our spirits twined together in a holy union of Love that rocked my being from Heaven to Earth, and all I could do was breathe her name, beautiful Mary, the Magdalene, the daughter of the Goddess.

She came toward me to take my hand. She, being Mary, laughed. She threw back her head and her golden-red curls washed down her back. I could hear her laughter, like music, like chimes in the wind. She said, "Oh, Jeshua, rise up and come to me as we have always been — two who know each other as one heart beating. Always have and always will. There's no need to make a fuss."

She, carrying all that feminine wisdom, knew what was in my heart and she knew, as I did, our path together and what it meant. I knew that we were meant to be together and that the work I came to do was nothing without her. We were and have always been one living whole, and only with her could I speak with God's true voice.

Looking into each other's faces, she reached out her hand to me. I was still awestruck and continued to kneel there, completely beyond the ability to make words. All I could do was barely catch my breath and reach my hand out to her. The moment that she took my hand we were merged, never to be apart again. As our fingers met, I exploded into the most exquisite experience of Light. I became truly the great Divine Masculine, totally aware of her as that which I needed to bring balance and to bring true life and vision to my heart. I knew she was as necessary to me as water, as sunlight, as breathing. I knew I was part of her as well.

With that touch, the Light of our hearts blended, and I was exploded back into the Halls of God. I saw the whole circle of our being and how we had chosen to be the voice of the One. I also knew what would be when we came together, body, mind, soul and spirit. Holding within our beings the Light of Our Beloved Creator, we were meant to light every heart on Earth.

I also knew the power of our Love-Making even though we had done no more than touch. I could see and feel the energy between us building, resonating so strongly it felt the Earth was shaking. The Light was brighter than even my greatest meditations and I could feel our spirits dancing in joy. Every atom of our bodies was vibrating in expectation, in recognition and magnetic presence. I knew that our coming together would be like a comet whose blazing light was a sign for God.

Oh, the truth is, even then I had no idea! It was, indeed, more than I ever could have imagined. But right then, holding her hand and gazing at her was such an intense experience and such an amazing gift that I was filled. It was more than enough. My heart simply said, "God, thank You. I am humble in my gratitude to You for bringing me this gift."

In that moment our spirits returned to their conscious union and have never been apart since. Not that we could ever truly be separate, but we had moved outward in our service to God, that we might embrace the living whole as we came together.

This was the year when I was twenty-two by the counting of the world. The energies of the body's awakening were strong within me as well as the fire that continually burned for God. I knew that we should not wait, that our merging was an affirmation of what was to come and Mary knew it too.

We barely said a word to each other because everything was in our heart and in our eyes. We exchanged, unspoken, our deep commitment to being this living flame of Love, the candle to light the way for all humanity back to unity. Because we were awake and I had not faltered in my remembrance of the living Holy One, we also knew the divine plan and our service, and we knew our time was short.

We spent the rest of that day walking through the streets of Jerusalem. She took me to the Temple of Women where she was studying and showed me the beautiful gardens and especially the grand view of the sky. As the sun set, we murmured our Love songs to each other and knew that something new was being born, that we were about to encounter a mystery beyond anything yet experienced.

As we sat in the garden, we spoke of it and we talked about the laws of the world. We talked about the judgment of egos and of the various religions. We both acknowledged the truth of our hearts, which was that we were already joined. We consciously agreed to be together in body as well as spirit, for we knew our God as a God of Love in which every aspect of life is embraced, in which nothing can be other than sacred, as long as God is fully honored.

Our hearts had said to us always that we were married in the Real of Love. We agreed that what happened with our bodies would simply enhance what was true of our spirits and already had been born into the world as we joined every night when we weren't together and worshiped God with our Love.

That night we met in the shadow of the Goddess Temple. Beside it we could look up at the stars and watch them wheeling overhead in all of their glory. It was the perfect inspiration, the perfect setting, because we were also aware that we were anchoring a whole new energy into the world. With our coming together, a new life was emerging for humanity, a true remembrance.

The seed of our Love would be sprouting for at least 2000 years, but we knew that it must be planted now by our Love, by that Temple. It was the new order of life supplanting the old, the parting of the veil of fear and prejudice and the coming of the true awakened vision of the living God as everything.

As the stars danced above us and the stones of the Temple gave off the day's heat, on the dust we laid our blanket and came together. It was beyond my greatest imagining, for as our hearts merged, it was pure ecstasy and the whole of Creation opened to us. We were our glorious vastness ever singing our heart's devotion to the One. All the while our spirits danced in remembrance of this great merging that was ever occurring.

For those who might be disconcerted by our physical merging before some sort of vows on Earth were said, please let me deeply reassure you that our marriage had long before occurred in the realms of Light and was intimately blessed by God, Him/Herself. The bells of Heaven were ringing that night when we came together in the shade beneath the moonlight by the Temple of Women, and on our blanket under the stars, we knew our marriage was truly omni-dimensional in all realms of God.

Mary and I also knew that our marriage would manifest on the physical plane at the right time, the right place, the right pattern as an expression of what had already occurred in the realms of Love. And so it did, many times, in different ways. We were first handfasted by the Essenes, witnessed in a great circle by their whole community. Later we were joined in a public ceremony in Jerusalem, observed by our families and all of our friends. Then again, in our travels, in a cave in India — a berm of Earth into which we climbed — we were blessed by a holy man who was aligned with the Buddha.

You must also remember that we lived in a time when the culture of the Goddess was still very strong in the people and the ways of the Goddess were widely celebrated. Even among the Hebrews, the Jews, the spirit of Shekinah, the Divine Feminine, was experienced and worshiped.

The Song of Solomon provides an accurate picture of relationships of the time. The emergence of patrilineal culture and the deep roots of the matrilineal created a wide array of attitudes and forms of relationship and marriage. Marriage was mainly focused around the joining of families and dynasties.

Much of what has been attributed to Christianity was simply not present in the outlook of the people of those times. While men of the Hebrews were pushing hard for their laws and views, children were as yet still seen as gifts from the Goddess to women. Sexuality was celebrated. I say this so you won't allow the views of your times to close you to the very sacred and powerful energies awakening in Mary and me together.

Our bodies coming together brought the joining of every atomic structure we are given for the purpose of creating for God. The great orgasmic joy of our Love-Making was so vast and so complete that the physical merging was impossible to separate from all the rest, as our beings were reunited. In truth, it was the full remembrance of who we are as each other's heart, as one being in God, one heart ever giving Love together.

We saw and felt the Angels who were attending us and a greater and more holy union has never occurred. The golden Light of Mary's atoms dancing merged with the pure Light of mine and every single one became a flame of God remembrance as we experienced our Real heart. I looked at my beloved Mary Magdalene, she who had been trained in the Goddess teachings, she who knew all the ways of Making Love. She was as overwhelmed and completely stunned as I.

We knew that what we were experiencing was far beyond us. It was the coming together of Earth and sky, of the world and the living spirit — the remembrance of the great Divine Masculine and Divine Feminine whose Real bodies are the body of God, the living Light expressing itself forever in Love.

While it is difficult to explain in words the beauty or the power or the absolute awe and amazement, I can say to you that it was a total merging. Every part of our beings were one — heart, spirit and body. We were whole. The whole night was spent in this divinity. Where our bodies left off and our spirits began was indistinguishable. Whether we merged again and again in the physical was beyond notice because our hearts and spirits and living Love kept coming together. Everything we are was a hymn to the One, to the Creator to whom we gave our hearts and beings.

We saw very clearly our pattern and purpose and acknowledged the Resurrection to come. We also at last spoke the truth we were feeling which was that nothing could ever come between our merging, not even the release of the body of one of us, because we had remembered our true Love-Making, and we knew that it goes on and on forever. We are One.

God spoke into my heart as God always did and said, "I anoint you as the living vehicle for the birth of true Christ Consciousness, as the wholeness of Divine Masculine and Divine Feminine, my beloveds." I said these words to Mary as they came to me, and she acknowledged that she heard the same voice. As the dawn came and we watched the sky becoming light, we talked about those things that we had intuited about our path together, our life of service and the things that we had been shown that night.

The clearest vision that we received together was the awareness of the moment of my transformation. When that moment came, the pulsing of our one heart and all that we would learn in the years before us would help us hold the pattern of our being, while I had the experience of dying. The energies of our being and our true resonance would hold the pattern clearly without faltering.

I could reassemble the molecules from the atoms by communicating God's Will to them and with my beloved Mary's assistance, I could build the body of Christ made new through the Will of God's Love. This body would be the new body for humanity, made of pure and totally conscious Light, joined as Divine Masculine and Divine Feminine in Paradise on Earth. This was what we were on Earth to anchor together, and our hearts, our beings, all we are was saying "Yes."

As we rose that morning hand-in-hand and folded our blanket, the feeling in my heart was pure ecstasy and I had a clarity of vision that I had never had before, even with all my connection to the Creator. When I looked at beautiful Mary, I was overcome with Love.

I said to her, "Mary, I can't be parted from you, not ever again, now that we have returned to our unity." She laughed and said, "Don't worry. The spirit is everything and even if we are to be separate at times in body, we will never really be separate again. I am in you and you are in me; you are my beloved, my beautiful Jeshua and I walk in your footsteps from now on, as you dance in mine."

Then I laughed, because Mary had always been poetic and she spoke now in words that were beyond the greatest human rhyme. I could feel the vibration of the living spirit in them, and I could feel her unique and genuine Love. I knew what a blessing God had given my being by providing me with her.

*May you see and feel the light of the Beloved
looking through your eyes and gazing
at you wherever you go,
whatever you do,
and in every reflection
of the created world.*

Chapter Four

"We greet you as the Christos..."

In the realms of God only Love exists. Only Love is Real. Only Love has substance, and Light is Love's movement. To me, the world looked completely different than it does to you, for I did not see the world through the eyes of ego. I saw the world only as the Christ, as the heart of God, pure and perfect. Those things that plague humanity were like a mist to me. At this point in my life I did not fully understand my destiny. But what I did understand was the truth of Love that radiated from my heart and I found the truth of Love in every being whom I encountered.

When I would see people standing before me, what I saw was the truth of their soul. I saw the beauty of their heart. I saw them as God made them. I saw them as an extension of the Creator's Love, whole and perfect, according life as joy. This is what I saw when I looked at them, and so they saw it too. This is the truth of all healing. It is the recognition, soul-to-soul, that all the rest is like the mist that rises over a lake in the morning and has no substance in the realms of Light.

For those who could look into my eyes and heart and see their own truth shining, my presence in the world was a reminder of what had been forgotten for so long. Because of this truth, lepers were healed and people who were crippled could pick up their beds and walk. I never did anything but see the truth in everyone.

To me the reality of my relationship with Mary was completely in harmony with the truth of Love, for Love, when you see with the eyes of spirit, is like sunlight glistening as it touches the human countenance and reveals what lies within. This was the truth of my life and my heart.

I knew that even the slightest ripple of Love from a human heart is noticed in the realms of truth and is given the greatest importance. All the rest, all the struggles and deceit, all the lies and the murders — none of it really registers in the realms of the Creator. This might seem shocking to some of you. Yet, the truth is that it was my coming that brought into the world a means of deeper communication for the living spirit of Love with the reality of life in the world. But this had not occurred at this time of which I speak.

So I danced across the fields of Creation in innocence and loved my beloved with all my heart and soul and being, and it was perfect. Remember, before you place the judgments of the world upon us, that I lived totally in the truth of Love. Knowing that only Love is important, I honored it always. And yet, though our Love was born in the realms of grace and purity, my beloved was to teach me many things about earthliness, about living a life that rejoiced in the physical things — in the beauty of the grass beneath our feet and the sun upon our skin; the touch of water, cool upon our hands; the taste of fruit; holding the Light and making it available as nutrition.

I began to understand how sunlight was captured and made into the forms that created this world. While I had always lived life steeped in spiritual truth, it wasn't until I came together with my beloved

Mary, the Magdalene, that I gained any real consciousness of physical life. Oh, she taught me so many things! The earth was our honeymoon suite. We walked upon the hillsides as we journeyed toward my parents in Nazareth, for the first thing I wanted to do was bring her home to them.

We traveled slowly and on foot so we could take in everything and bring it into our hearts and rejoice in it. Thus it was that one midnight found us entering Galilee and sitting together upon a hilltop in silence. We felt the presence of the energies of life as they moved in the world and sang in the voices of insects and sheep and danced in the shimmering leaves of the olive trees. In the moonlight we could see the forms of the sheep like white circles of light in the darkness. The furrows in the field were shadows upon the tableau of the rolling hills that were my home.

As we sat upon that hilltop and felt the resonance of the living Word rising within us, I reached out and took my beloved's hand and said, "Watch! We have visitors." I felt them deep within before I saw them, and I knew them well. Slowly there coalesced out of the darkness two great streams of Light that stood before us with the energies of the Angels I knew so well. To honor us in our earthly walk, they took on forms similar to ours, although made completely of Light.

The first Angel spoke. You would not know her name for she is not someone who regularly works with the Earth but I knew her well, for the realms of Creation were open to me. She bowed and said, "We greet you as the Christos. We bring you tidings of the pure Light of the Creator. We recognize and honor your service to humanity."

As the second Angel spoke, the darkness grew lighter. His countenance shone with a light greater than the sun. I recognized the power of a glorious Archangel, the one whom you know as Michael, champion of humanity.

When he spoke, the whole world reverberated. All the sheep stopped in their tracks and looked up. Every bird was silent. Night noises ceased as the insects held their breath and waited.

In a voice that resonated within our beings and literally shook us to every atom, Michael said to me, "Hail to the living Christos. I am here always to assist you. I am the champion of humanity and I am the protector of all the precious hearts in the world, defender of their purity, of their hope. Know that I shall always be here to serve you for I have known the two of you as one heart of Love eternally."

I found surprise in the tears upon my cheek as my heart responded to his passion and commitment. I said to him, "I, too, am the champion of humanity and I join myself with you, beloved Michael, in making it my will that their freedom be complete. I promise to remain with them until it is true." He bowed to me and said, "This is accepted in the Halls of God."

I turned to look at Mary and as she looked at me, her eyes were shining and tears were on her face as well. I squeezed her hand, and I noticed how the olive trees were actually reaching out their branches toward Michael and the Angel who stood beside him. As they reached for the nourishment of his grand and powerful Light, their voices whispered, "We know you."

I marveled within myself that there was so much consciousness everywhere I looked in the world. Every form of life remembered the truth of our Creator. Deep within every life is the memory of living in perfect harmony with God and making of the world the conscious paradise that was the original intention.

I turned once again to the almost blinding Light that is Michael, and bowed my head to him in honor. I felt his sword of truth rest upon me like an arrow puncturing my aura and bringing a bolt of Light so powerful it shook me. It brought back in utter clarity the eternal joy that is the Angels as they hold the energy of truth for everyone.

The first Angel spoke again and said to both of us, "You are the womb of Love in time, bringing the Light of God, our Creator, to humanity through your great heart. We now accord this, that you might bring to birth these gifts for the world. You are to build the living grid of Light as you concur with all the Masters of Light on Earth and consciously create the true divinity of living Love for the world.

"The opening you will bring to the dream of life on Earth will allow the Creator's Light to penetrate the world — accomplished by the transformation of your body into the eternal body of Light you truly wear. Within your greater heart is the womb of Love, a Star of Love that will entrain the hearts of humankind. Ultimately, there will also be the conception of a child, a daughter, whose DNA of Light will plant the rebalancing of the feminine for humankind and the birth of a new form of human being whose orientation shall be as yours — the realms of truth, Light and Love, and not the world of dreams."

Her voice fell into the silence. We sat there while the night was lit up around us and the vibration of living Light from the Angels lifted our bodies and made of them pure Light as well. We were suspended between the world and the realms of Light in a space of silence and peace, and we were filled with the Love of our Creator, made manifest before us as the Angels and the living truth they carry.

The passage of time ceased to exist for us. I had no idea of how long we were there, simply drinking in the true nourishment from our Creator and feeling the attunement of our shared heart with God's glory. When at last I felt a nudge from the Creator who always spoke within me through my heart, I opened my eyes, surprised to see the dawn's Light rising all around us. As dawn came stealing across the hills drenching the olive trees slowly in Light, their leaves became a golden salute to morning.

Suddenly there was the voice of all the birds. As always I could hear what they were saying. Their song is a hymn of worship, worship of the living moving whole of Love in which they always live and are forever singing. It was a song of joy in the glory of the sunlight holding for the world the essence of the Real Light that is ever our nourishment and the source of our energy.

The grass turned suddenly from shadow to perfect green. The sheep grazed, beautiful in the morning Light. Everything was shining, dew-drenched and perfect for we had been bathed in grace by the visit of the Angels. Pulling Mary down with me, I lay back on the grass and felt my body as insubstantial. It had never been for me very physical, for as I said to you, it was an octave above the world. And yet, it allowed me to experience the life that humanity lived.

This morning I felt like Light incarnate, though I could see the shape of my body on the grass. What I did feel as substantial was Mary's hand in mine. When I rolled over to her, the look on her face was a look of complete delight and joy. I had met the experience of the Angels with a hymn to God and a feeling of reverence, but she, drinking in the gift of their presence, had made of it a feast of joy, an enhancement of the richness of her life on Earth and all the ways that she loved it.

Suddenly her laughter rang out and rolled across the hill like an echo. Her hair was spread out behind her on the grass. I tenderly touched her face. She placed my hand upon her heart and said, "Oh, Jeshua, what a miracle this is — all of it so amazing, so incredible, so delicious. Don't you love it? Look. Feel it." She took my hand then and placed it on the Earth. She said, "Can you not feel that the Earth has a heartbeat too and She too is grateful for the Angels' visit?"

As I listened, I heard it. It was the rhythm that I knew so well echoing the heartbeat of Creation, like a signal being sent of Love received and accorded. I placed my hand upon her heart again and suddenly I was seeing the world through Mary's eyes. It was different from how I saw the world, which was as many shades and movements of Light and the visible expressions of Love. The world I saw as I blended with Mary was a rich jewel box, jewel tones drenched in the living sunlight and radiating out joy. Everything was so clear, so defined, so vibrant and colorful that it moved me to my core. I recognized in that moment how much Mary had to teach me about living the paradise that was held in trust for humanity.

We lay there in the sunlight for many hours, taking in our nourishment directly, and we accorded the life in the olive trees as we felt them communing with us. I breathed in a new awareness of life as seen by humanity with eyes open to the beauty, expressed in a richness that I had never seen before. Eventually we rose and as we held hands, the fire between us leaped and burned. Our spirits rose in glorious ecstasy as once again we blended and worshiped the Creator together.

The moment passed as such moments did. I had come to recognize that there were waves in this life on Earth that continually surprised me with their intensity, waves that lifted me to the highest and then returned me back to the world. I had learned how to simply flow with these waves and to let them have their way with me. I recognized that it was a way of bringing the energy back and forth from the highest realms of Light into the world and back again. Knowing always that I was an instrument for the Creator, I honored it.

"My beloved," I said, "it's time to go visit my parents." "So it is," she said, and laughing, she left me and began to run straight down that hillside as the sun rose toward noon. Laughing, too, I ran behind her. I realized as I ran that I lived always absorbed in the Light. Feeling the Earth energy moving as I ran was exhilarating. I thought, another gift from Mary.

We ran all the way to the bottom of the rolling hills and then stopped to catch our breath. At that very moment there came a cart pulled by a donkey and sitting on it a man I knew very well. It was my childhood friend whose name was Judas. "My, aren't you looking bright this morning……" he said to me. And then he looked at Mary and smiled. With a rumble in his chest that I knew was a laugh, he said, "Aha, Jeshua is in Love! I can hardly believe it, but it is obviously true." I smiled in turn and said, "My dear friend Judas, I want you to meet my beloved." They bowed to each other in greeting. When Judas looked up, he said, "Don't I know you? Aren't you that little girl who used to harass Jeshua, and didn't the two of you picnic in the hills?" Both of us together were laughing as we told him, "Oh, yes, that was us."

"Hop in," he said, or an equivalent in the language of our times. We laughed and talked all the way home as I told him some of the high points of my travels and told him simply that Mary and I had met in Jerusalem. When he pulled up before the house of my guardians, my beautiful and beloved Mary and Joseph, he looked me in the eye very seriously, and said, "Jeshua, I know you and I know this is for real and I am glad. If there is anything you ever need, I am here for you. You know I am always your friend."

I gripped his arm and he gripped mine in a grasp of brotherhood. I noted how strong he had become, how he had grown into a man who was quite formidable and certainly quite handsome. His dark eyes snapped and danced in the Light and his hair, almost black, shone in the sun. His beard was thick and neatly trimmed and he was definitely a presence. He noticed me inspecting him and laughed again and said, "Not the little boy any more, am I?" "Not at all," I said. "And what about you? Are you in Love?" "Oh," he jokingly said, "I'll just take Mary. She's beautiful." Of course, I said to him the equivalent of "no way." With warmth, we parted.

I turned with Mary toward the door of the humble home of my childhood. Before we even raised our hand to knock, the door burst open and there my mother stood, radiant in her beauty that was so delicate and at the same time so strong. Her eyes, like mine, were blue though hers had flecks of hazel. Her rich dark auburn hair as yet hung down, which was very unusual in our neighborhood where all the married women wore their hair tightly bound and mostly covered. She did have on her headpiece, the cloth she wore, but the tendrils of her hair still fell everywhere.

For the first time I recognized her physical beauty as a woman as well as my guardian. I knew that this, too, was a gift from my Mary, the one also known as the Magdalene. She had given me a new view of the world and all the life in it. It was now so much more "real" to me than it had ever been before. Quickly I was in my mother's arms and she was in mine, and we hugged each other exuberantly. Our hearts simply acknowledged our enduring and eternal connection.

With a start, my mother looked over my shoulder and saw my beloved standing there. With an indrawn breath, she said, "Oh my goodness, there she is." She hollered out, "Joseph, come here. It has happened." Joseph came quickly, almost running, with a big smile across his face. His beard had grown longer than ever. I could see that he had aged and yet, to me, he still looked so vibrant and so handsome, so steadfast in his support and his Love for my mother, Mary.

He moved right beyond me and ran to clasp my beloved in a great hug of welcome. As he laughed in delight, he looked from me to my Mary and back again and he said, "Aha, your mother is right. But then she always is……" He hugged me and grabbed both of our hands and pulled us quickly into the house. In the cool shadows of the main room in which we lived I felt enveloped in welcome. It felt so good to be home. Before I knew it, my mother had scurried around and brought us food, and we sat down together at the wooden table that had been so lovingly built by Joseph. Laughing and talking, sharing our story, we ate together. Mary was wrapped in the Love of my family and just like that, she was part of it.

After our meal I went with Joseph to the woodshop where he showed me his projects. They were beautiful. When we returned, I ask about the other children who were, in essence, my brothers and sisters, although their conception had been different and their lives were more physical. While I was briefed on what had been happening in the time I had been gone, my heart just soaked up the contentment. As the day waned, the talk turned to the spiritual and I shared with them the visit by the Angels.

My mother clasped her hands across her chest and said, "Oh, I am so glad. Isn't it the most incredible experience?" "It's beyond words," I said. Then my beloved Mary spoke and shared her perspective, and my guardians, my mother and father of my Earth life, listened carefully with so much respect for her that I was truly overjoyed.

Then, with a sudden bustle and lots of noise, the door flew open and my sister and brothers rushed in. There were three other children in this family that Love built and by now, they were teenagers and their presence filled up that house to overflowing as they rushed to Mary and Joseph for their hugs. Spotting me, they started shouting with excitement, "Jeshua, Jeshua, Jeshua is here!" Soon I was in a tumble of embracing arms and kisses on both cheeks. I thought, happiness comes in so many forms, doesn't it? What a moment and what a miracle!

As soon as I could get a word in, I said, "Do you remember Mary? She is now the Magdalene." "You are?" my sister said, and suddenly she belonged to Mary for she had been always drawn to the Goddess Temple. She went to Mary's side and she stayed there. In every moment that I would let her, she was asking my beloved Mary a hundred questions. Mary seemed delighted to answer her and to share with her what had occurred in her years of study. My brothers, on the other hand, were smitten with Mary and completely overwhelmed by her beauty and they made comments to that effect. I laughingly informed them that she was mine, that we had bonded beyond the world, and that they would have to look elsewhere for their entertainment. We all laughed together.

So began a time of simplicity, peace and contentment where Mary and I were wrapped in my family's Love as we got into the rhythm of the days as they were in that simple house in Nazareth. We pitched in right away and did our share of what needed doing, and I spent hours in the shop with Joseph. Soon the word had spread that I was home in Nazareth and so was Mary, who once had lived there and was now the Magdalene. Like lightning the word was passed that we were together, that we were betrothed, that we would be hand-fasted in the Essene community and married later in Jerusalem, honoring all traditions. This part people didn't necessarily understand but they honored it.

*Let the stars point the way
in the midst of this outer darkness,
for there is a voice
within your heart
whispering and
calling your name.*

Chapter Five

"These are the hands of the Goddess here on Earth..."

As the days went by, I could tell that my beloved was becoming comfortable at being enfolded by my family. This enfolding Love recognized our Love together and honored it deeply and respectfully. While she might not have admitted it, I could tell that this was important to her.

Our days were very busy assisting in all the things there were to do to keep the household running and the family happy. Ah, but in the evenings as the sun went down, it was my favorite time. We gathered around the table for our evening meal and afterwards, when the dishes were cleared, we began to converse together about those things that were important to my heart. We had always done this, even when I was a child, and even when my brothers and sister were children. Mary and Joseph understood that children are very open to the living awareness of our Creator and thus we were always invited to participate in the discussion of spiritual matters.

In the evenings, my Mary and I would sit together, very close, our knees touching, and holding hands, while the family gathered. We lit the lamps and began to share our deepest feelings about God. I remember one night in particular that touched me deeply. As we began to speak, the room stilled and even my siblings were suddenly quiet. We could feel the atmosphere change.

The air around us became brighter and clearer. Then, out of the silence came a sound like great wings and a song arose like a whisper of pure Love. It increased in volume and intensity as other Heavenly voices were added. The whole atmosphere became filled with a chorus of Angels. As my heart moved and opened in rejoicing, rising to the call of the Heavenly song, I glanced around the table and every face was washed in tears. Every head was tilted back, eyes focused upward, although there was really nothing to see — only to hear. The rising movement of the Heavenly chorus lifted us all into the cosmic splendor that is ever present and waiting for us to feel it.

We were suspended beyond time in the eternal present with our very deepest spirits rejoicing in a song so rich and so endless that it brought back the memories of our communion with the living moving spirit of God as our Mother and our Father. The Love within the music was so palpable and the feeling of God's presence so near that we could only respond to the tender intimacy of the relationship that is waiting for us all. Everywhere we look and all we feel and see is a doorway to this tender sharing because each of us is the living child of the great Love that created us.

When the music began to fade, our vision returned to normal and breaths that had been held began to breathe again. Without conscious volition we reached out and joined hands and simply sat, heads bowed in a circle in reverence. When at last it was time to speak, what we spoke of was the miracle of the intimacy of the Creator's Love and how our beloved

Creator tenderly tends us in every moment of our life. We spoke of how so many had forgotten this and saw God as something far removed. We spoke of the dedication of our hearts to bringing to humankind the remembrance of this communion that is so intimate and so real. It is the Creator's greatest gift waiting to be recognized.

I encourage you who hold these pages in your hand to accord this miracle for yourself. Open your heart and consciousness to God's tender Love as your cosmic Mother and Father, as well as the living breathing hologram of endless Love in which you live.

While at first it seemed in that evening of such amazing grace that we could barely speak, let alone of worldly things, eventually we began to talk of more concrete ways that we felt we could go into the world and serve, and light the candle of the remembrance of God's presence in every heart. Until this moment my beloved Mary had been mostly silent, her eyes shining with unshed tears. Her face was holding a look of bemused awe and she was glowing. She truly took my breath away whenever I looked at her, but of course, I was aware of her every moment.

When at last she spoke, the words she said were so profound that it brought silence once again to our table. She held out her hand to each of us in turn and said, "These are the hands of the Goddess here on Earth. These are the hands by which She shall show the world that She is truly here, tender and intimate. What I do, I do as She moves through my heart, and opens up my conscious eyes to see, that I might serve her precious children as all of us in unity."

Once again our heads were bowed in acknowledgement of the truth that my beloved spoke. All together our hearts rose up in response to the gift given to us by the Angels, not only of their song that was so majestic and so beautiful, but the gift of what it brought to our conversation, to our hearts and to our consciousness. And so it was that we passed every evening in a similar way until the evening came when the subject was approached of my beloved and my departure for the community of the Essenes. I could see immediately how disappointed my mother, Mary, was, and I could see the longing in Joseph's eyes. I knew that as my parents they wanted nothing more than to keep us home with them.

I also knew that they understood the call of the living God that lived and moved and dwelled within my being, and who sang before me as my beloved Mary's Love and called me forth in service. I said to them, "My heart is speaking to me in that endless voice of the Creator's Love and says to me that we must go forth to weave all past, all philosophies, all religions into one tapestry of worship for the living God. That living moving harmony of grace and Love that tends us, guides us and loves us also lifts us up and gives us a greater vision that shows all of humankind as the holy child, waiting to be free."

Joseph bowed his head in acknowledgement and then looked at me. "My son, who is also the Christos, I have always known the path before you and that this time would come. You have been absent as much as you've been home. Yet, I will miss you so much, and the parent I am cannot help but wish that you could stay. But, Jeshua and Mary, you know that we will always and forever support you. We will be here with you when the time comes for the closing of the era and the awakening to a new potential for humanity that shall be brought to Earth by you, Jeshua. We will meet easily in the realms of spirit.

"Remember all that we have taught you — that you can travel with the speed of Light as you command the atoms of your body with God power." Reaching out he took my both my hands in his, and looking me deep in the eyes, he said, "Promise me, Jeshua, that you will use these tools. For I know that you already have accomplished this. Promise me you will come to see your mother and me, that you will materialize in the night and set our hearts to rest."

Squeezing his hand, I said, "Dearest Joseph, my guardian, my father as I walk upon this Earth, I promise, and I will teach my beloved to travel in the realms of Light. We will be here many many times. But I also ask you to come and see us as well. Come and bless us in our nights." He said that he would.

Then I laughed and said, "What is all this seriousness? You know we are going to see you shortly, and we will see you again before we leave for all of our travels. Something is coming to me about Jerusalem, so I think there are still many times ahead of us for coming together as a family and spending this wonderful time sharing all that we are." Joseph began to laugh with me and so did my mother. My mother said, "It's just that we know so much of what is to come, and sometimes my mother's heart leaps out before me and wants to pull you back and keep you close."

I said, "Dearest and beautiful mother, vessel of the Angels, holder of purity and a mother's Love for the world, I bless you and I recognize who you are. I am so honored to have been graced by your mother's Love. I promise I will always honor you and I will be here with you every possible moment I can. I will take every opportunity. I also ask you to come to our side and to honor our official joining when we are handfasted with the Essenes."

She nodded her beautiful head and I watched the dancing Light that shone like a golden halo about her. I marveled at her beauty and her majesty and the power that was held in such a feminine body. In that moment, time opened for me and I saw the world with every Age blended into one. I saw my mother, Mary, holding them all like a mother holds a child. I really saw her for what she is, not through a child's eyes or even a peer, but with the reverent eyes of one who sees the face of the Creator as the majestic and eternal feminine and as the Mother's Love.

The beauty of this vision took my breath away and I actually shook my head to clear it, and found myself incapable of making words. So I simply held her hand, my mother, and marveled at who she is and at the honor of being with her.

And so it was that we began to prepare for our journey, for the summer was waning and the time was right. We had received the guidance rising from within that we were to be joined by the Essene community on the Equinox, that time that came right after the Jewish holiday of Sukkot, a time of celebration of the harvest and a time of gratitude for our bounty. It was the perfect time to be married.

With my parents' help, we gathered together the things that we would need and made plans for our journey toward Mt. Hermon and the Essene community. While we had spoken that evening of traveling in spirit, I had not had time yet to instruct my beloved Mary, and so we discussed how we would travel. Would we hire a cart with a donkey? Would we allow Judas to take us, for, of course, he had offered. Or would we choose to walk?

Mary's vote was to walk because she loved the Earth. She loved to feel it beneath her feet and to worship the Goddess within it and within all the expressions of nature. While I tended to agree with her for I, too, loved to walk everywhere, I was also aware that we needed to take a cart, for it was the protocol to arrive bearing gifts of gratitude and honoring the household that would take you in. Since the community of the Essenes was a very large household, I felt the desire to bring them many things in an expression, in symbols, of our gratitude and our excitement at being joined by them.

Ultimately we decided to travel with Judas. He and Mary could get to know each other, and he and I could have time to honor our connection as spiritual brothers. We began our journey on a day where the Light had begun to change. It was one of those days where you can just feel a shift and you know that the seasons are turning. In the sunlight that seemed to fall with a different flavor that day, I could have sworn that the particles of Light dancing were different. Saluting them, I climbed with my beloved into the cart being guided by Judas, and we all squeezed together on the bench seat. Saying goodbye to my family, we welcomed a new chapter in our journey.

While our travels were wonderful, what stands out most of all was the time with Judas. There are so many accounts of who he was. I would like to share with you my account. Judas was and is my dearest heart brother. From the day we first played together as children, we have always known what we shared — a deep commitment of brotherhood that went beyond any life in the world, and way beyond the shadow dance of the dramas of human life.

Both of us had spoken often of our deep desire to fulfill that mission that called from within us. Even as children we had joined our palms and made a pact to always obey the spirit's voice and to honor our bond above everything else, while sharing our service to God.

Judas had shared many meals with my family and joined in many of the sundown discussions. But even more than this, he and I had spent day after day wandering through the hills and the fields of Galilee and speaking from our hearts. We had had experiences of deep revelation, and had seen glimpses of what was to come. Both of us knew that what we were called to do was going to be difficult if we saw it as human beings — but not if we held our consciousness in the pure Light and our hearts accorded only the greater truth that Love is all there truly is, the only thing that is Real. We loved each other and we loved God.

As we traveled on our way to the Essene community, Judas and Mary and I spoke of these things. As we did, the spirit moved within us and brought forth our mission more clearly. We began to take turns speaking what was being revealed to us, knowing that it was the Creator's voice. First, Judas spoke and said, "I see the drama unfolding that will bring to you the opportunity to transform every old idea of limited humanity into the glory of the spirit. But I also feel a terrible weight bearing down. It is the weight of a judgment of history. I play a part in this drama, my brother, my Jeshua, and I fear it is going to be very very difficult."

Not being one to skirt around the truth revealed, I clasped his arm, for I was sitting next to Judas, and said, "I too have seen some of this in my silence and I acknowledge it will be challenging. But, Judas, I know who you are. You know me and you know that we are brothers always — brothers of the heart — and nothing will ever change this. I want you always to remember this, and remember that we are here to create an opening for life and Love. This is truly our mission and nothing else."

Then my beloved spoke and said, "I see my part as well. I see myself holding the Light for both of you, according the truth of your beings with all that I am, and keeping that vibration going through all the swirling energies around us as we allow the unfolding of the drama that will bring about this anchoring of the Christos for humanity."

I could feel the tension leave Judas as Mary spoke. I recognized how important it was to him to know that he had assistance through a woman's heart who would hold him in perfection as we allowed the patterns to unfold through us. I clasped Mary's hand in my right as I held Judas' arm in my left. I sat between the two of them, and the Love poured through my open heart to them.

Around us the Love became vibrant and palpable until we could feel its living pulsations, that shimmering pulse beat that keeps the rhythm of Creation for us. The Love pouring through my heart enveloped all of us, and we felt the dynamic presence of our Creator. Each of us felt the reassurance from God, both within us and all around us, and we knew with a vision born of the realms beyond time that our mission would be successful and we were satisfied.

Oh, that I could send an arrow
of divine thought
straight into your heart
that you might see the light
and the love
streaming forth
from the life within you!

Chapter Six

"We can place ourselves anywhere we choose on the line of time..."

The sacred ocean of unity in which we live has one heartbeat, one breath and one ever-present movement of Love. It has one Light that shines out from the center. This very Light is also the center of our being, for the whole of Creation is completely woven together.

All of this was completely open to me. I lived, breathing this one breath and feeling always that rhythm of Creation. My consciousness was awake to the rhythm of the unity that speaks through us all and reveals itself through heart and consciousness continually in the living present.

So it was that, as I walked the Earth, the path before me was revealed as I walked it. The living present that is the wholeness of God contains no concept of past and future. It might seem, as you listen to this narrative, that the future was veiled to me. But the truth is it was simply revealed in the moment as I lived it. If I had a need to see the greater pattern, I needed only to ask and it was there before me. Mostly, I was content to let the movement of the living spirit open up my service in the moment. I let it guide me, that living voice of Love within my heart, in perfect trust.

We approached the Essene community at Mt. Hermon, a place where I had spent many happy times.

Jochaim was the wise center of this community. He taught me much. Each Essene community was an entity in itself because each revolved around the person at the center, the one chosen to be the conduit of the pure Light of the Creator and to hold the space of Love for the living presence of the Christ that I bring.

The Essenes had been waiting for the coming of the Christos into the world. When the Creator spoke and told them that I was holding this, they accorded this truth as a living miracle. I had much to do to explain to them that it wasn't "me." I am only that which lives in every being, and thus I am a doorway for every heart into the remembrance of its truth.

But with Jochaim, I had never felt the seeds of idolatry or confusion about the role and the Light that I carried. With him I had ever been completely comfortable and I cherished our relationship as one of equals. I had spent many nights when the community was sleeping, engaged in deep discussion with him about grace, about the purpose of the spirit, about the portents, and about that which was unfolding around us. I truly cherished these discussions.

So I approached the community with delight, excited to see my mentor again. Yet as my foot moved toward Jochaim's sanctuary, my consciousness accorded a new energy and I stopped and listened. As I stopped, my beloved and my dearest friend bumped into me because I stopped so suddenly. Both of them looked at me with confusion. "What is it? What are you doing, Jeshua?" they asked.

After holding the opening for the living spirit and engaging in the silence that is complete, I saw a greater view of the pattern of our handfasting. I took a breath, realizing the implications of what I was seeing and how it would affect my beloved. I turned, one foot upon the step and one foot yet upon the ground. I looked upon the countenance of my Mary and said simply, "There is a new energy that I am seeing that points us directly to Jerusalem. But, beloved Mary, let us give this some time. Let us go and speak to my dear friend, Jochaim, the one about whom I have spoken to you, and let us see what he tells us."

As I stood there I gazed out upon the rolling hills and noticed the autumn sun in the grass, as the winds blew the pastured rams and touched our cheeks and lifted us, especially Mary's beautiful hair. As I watched, the shepherds of the community were gathering up their local flock and I could see in the distance the lush gardens that supported this community. I remembered that these people, who were like a family to me, this community of those who held the Light, were focused on the land and on the spirit of the Earth and on the conscious practice of animal husbandry. They accorded every animal its due as a conscious being and placed communication front and center.

It was a community that was very joyous, that was filled with a sense of harmony. The sun was golden as it washed across the hillside and shone upon the larger form of Mt. Hermon that rose up behind the simple structures that made up the community. By this time I could hear a stirring within the building, whose doorway held a sign of the blending of Heaven and Earth into one. It conveyed a feeling inviting all to come in and worship or to spend time in deep communion with Jochaim or to take the time to sit in the silence and listen to the living spirit within.

Jochaim had heard us standing outside of his doorway. Suddenly the door was thrown open and beaming with a smile that reached from ear to ear, he threw open his arms and grabbed me. He literally pulled me in across the threshold and into his arms. Both of us were laughing in joy. He wrapped his slender arms tightly around me and said, "Oh, Jeshua, how glad I am to see you! How much I have missed you in those times of your travels! Ah, but Mary and Joseph kept me posted always. Come. Come in, my dearest son, and introduce me."

In that moment he turned and looked at Mary. On an indrawn breath, he said, "Oh, my, she is the one who shares your flame." I reached out and took my beloved's hand and together we stood before him, heads bowed. Jochaim, my mentor and my dear friend and the spiritual guide for this whole community, placed a hand on each of our heads and gave us the blessing of the living, endless unity of God. His blessing spoke to our hearts as he prayed that we would always live by that Light and hear the voice that speaks within All That Is, and live by it.

At the end of his prayer, Mary and I both said, "Yes. We dedicate ourselves to this One, this living breathing endless God of unity who is both masculine and feminine, who is our Mother and our Father." Then I reached out my hand, drawing toward us my dear friend, Judas, and introduced Judas and Jochaim, who, with a great hug and with true delight, welcomed him to the Essene community.

Then he turned to me and said, "Let us go to the sanctuary, all of us, for there is much we have to share and quickly, for I have known of your visit and the purpose of it, and I have many things to tell you." As the sun began to set, slanting its orange and gold colors across the threshold of the open doorway and through the windows, we walked through the building and into the room that had ever been preserved for silence and prayer. All around it on every side were chairs and cushions. In the front was a beautiful altar, made out of wood, constructed with simplicity, and yet truly beautiful. Upon this, burned a single candle, one Light to the one God.

As we took a moment to acknowledge our place in the hologram, I felt the unity among us building. Then Jochaim drew us into a circle and reached behind him for four pillows, encouraging us to sit down before the altar with him and so we did. As I looked at him, I thought to myself how changeless he was, how he had always appeared exactly the same. He had a long beard that reached to his chest and was threaded with silver, and hair that flowed down his back, hair that was filled with every color of white and silver and gray. Jochaim always had appeared timeless and so did he still appear to me.

When he spoke it was with a voice deep and resonant. His hands, whose fingers were long and delicate, continually reached for ours. Holding each of our hands in turn, he said, "You are here for a purpose. In the great wheel of the movement of time, this visit is important. Yet, that for which you have come is not given to me to do."

Before I could speak, he stopped me and continued. "Jeshua," he said, "we have been dearest friends and I your mentor, and this is why you have turned to me to be joined to your beloved. But as you are beginning to see, the pattern clearly places your handfasting in Jerusalem, which is the focus of your mission, of your service. Please don't be disappointed," he said to me, as he looked into my eyes, "for you are truly a son to me, and I love you and cherish you. But I must always do what the living spirit guides me to do, and I am guided to send you on, after you and I have shared what you have come to learn. This we can do quickly."

I became aware of a pressing silence from my beloved. I could feel her emotions. Very quickly they became heavy and agitated, and her aura began to muddy and swirl. Sharing a silent communion with Jochaim and a look of understanding with Judas, I turned my whole body to Mary. Taking her hand, I said, "My beloved, you who shine at the center of my universe, I see this greater pattern. It was only given to me when my foot connected with the doorway. But I acknowledge it and Jochaim is seeing it correctly. Yet, you and I have something important to learn from my dearest Jochaim, and then we can quickly move on to Jerusalem. I promise you that it will be fine."

I had never before seen Mary distraught. How it tugged at my heart and brought feelings that I had never experienced. I sent her waves of reassurance through my heart and watched as it filled her aura. Her agitation began to subside. I placed my hand on her beautiful forehead and poured the Light into her third eye, until at last her breath began to flow more evenly and her heartbeat came to a steady rhythm.

I drew her into my arms and held her tenderly, and said, "Mary. It will be fine. Trust the movement of the spirit within us. You know we must always follow as the spirit guides." She suddenly pulled away and looked into my eyes with determination and once again, with distress. She said, "Jeshua, there is no way we can make it to Jerusalem before the Equinox. I know," she said, adamantly, "that we are meant to be handfasted at the time of balance, at that moment when Heaven and Earth are in harmony and the days and nights are equal."

Sharing a glance again with Jochaim, I opened heart and consciousness to the Creator and said a prayer within, "Oh, glorious Creator, Who is the living movement of Heaven and Earth, move through me and speak to my beloved and show her the truth about time." Then the voice of the spirit moved from within me and said, "Mary, please listen. I will show you what we must do. The truth of time is a construct made by humans. I can lift us beyond it and speaking The Word of God-power from within us, we can easily travel to Jerusalem in plenty of time."

She looked at me incredulous and said, "You must be making a joke, right, Jeshua? There is no way that we can travel to Jerusalem on foot, in a cart with donkey, even if we were to acquire some of those beautiful horses that the Romans use, we still couldn't make it and get ready for our joining in time. It is impossible." Out of the corner of my eye I could see that Judas was in agreement with her. Yet, Jochaim and I saw a different perspective.

And so I said, "Jochaim, if you are open to it, can we show both Mary and Judas the truth about time?" As we listened within, both he and I, we received the inner "Yes," and I felt the vibration change instantly. That which appeared as a room, as a sanctuary, opened and became Light moving. Jochaim and I reached out and created a circle, holding Judas' and Mary's hands. We

65

began to breathe and sing the living Word that is the song of Creation. Holding it as our Will with the living Creator, as the movement of the spirit and of Love, we felt ourselves rising into the great Reality of the timeless and glorious spirit, the unity of Love, the Creator.

I spoke with the words of the spirit, "Mary, Judas, look! Look with the eyes within your heart." As we looked, we could see the universe around us, and the movement of the living spirit within it. We could see the endless dimensions of this glorious unity, as they wove the Light through all things. In the center of every living particle was the silence that accorded the living truth of God in everything. As we clung to this peace and silence, we experienced the unity, how everything that could happen in the bubble of life on Earth was happening all at once. Only from an open perspective, like this moment that we shared, could we see how the human mind created a funnel that limited this vast open and living miracle and created lines of time.

I whispered into Mary's and Judas' consciousness, "We can place ourselves anywhere we choose on the line of time and we can choose when we go to Jerusalem. We can choose the moment when we arrive. By the power of living Love and of the endless Light that lives within us, we can elongate the moments of time and be arriving at the community in Jerusalem with all the moments that we need to prepare for our handfasting."

Then, with Jochaim, I lifted into the pure and resonant realms of living Love and the presence of the Creator, and asking, I received the burst of the Creator's "Yes." I brought Mary and Judas and Jochaim with me until we focused on the pattern of the return of the Christ to the Earth. All of us saw together the opening of humanity to this possibility, beginning with me, across the Ages in a new line of time and possibilities. We accorded this pattern and in our spirits, agreed to be this Light, to be this conduit for endless Love.

In an instant, we returned to the perspective of our bodies sitting together in the sanctuary. Mary looked dazed and Judas, awed. I said to them, "We are joined now in a new way and I trust both of you to be my allies and my dearest friends, and you, Mary, to always share this Love as we do what the spirit wills and speak as unity into the hearts on Earth." Both of them said, "Yes," and suddenly the energy seemed to leave my beloved. She slumped against me, completely exhausted from the travels, from the chaos in her emotional body and from the stretch into a new consciousness she had just experienced.

We began to take care of those things that must be done, as caretakers of the vehicles of our bodies. After feeding all of us, Jochaim said to me, "Let me show Mary to your chambers and Judas to his, and then, Jeshua, let us spend time talking." So I began a communion of the greatest depth with my dear mentor, Jochaim. He spoke to me about the reality of humanity — how it felt to be a human being. He said to me that he could tell I had not experienced this by how I responded to Mary. I agreed with him.

He patiently explained to me how the world looked and how the emotions were so powerful that for many, they seemed to rise up and take over everything and cause reactions beyond control. He painted for me pictures of things I had experienced, but always from the outside, looking in. He was showing me that these discordant relationships and incidents that I had seen were the result of these emotions.

I looked with every part of me and thought I understood. I felt the deep compassion in my heart. Yet after it all, Jochaim took my hand and said to me, "Well, Jeshua, it is a beginning, but I can see you won't really understand until the end. But when you do, it will change everything." This is all he would say. I pried, cajoled, even begged him, but he would say no more. At last, with a sigh, I said, "Thy Will be done," speaking to my beloved Creator.

As the evening waned into morning, I rose from my pillow and at last went to the chamber I shared with Mary, my Magdalene. I lay beside her and pulled her up close to me, holding her tenderly, placing my hand gently around her and my other arm beneath her head. I cradled her as I lifted into that state of humming joy that is between the waking consciousness that lives in the world and the pure experience of unity that is our communion with the Creator.

In that place I felt the Creator's tender Love, both personal and intimate. I knew that at that point where God becomes our hearts is the miracle that gives us forever a relationship with our Creator that is the greatest blessing of our lives. I was filled with gratitude. I often didn't sleep but simply fed the electrons of my body from the Light, bringing them into attunement with The One that lives and breathes within my being. As I knew myself as the movement of the Creator's Love, I had everything I needed to express the Christos perfectly.

In the morning, the whole community had discovered that I was inside, and there was much ado. Many blessings were coming through me and Mary as we opened to Love's movement. We at last prepared to depart with Judas, heading South again, back through Nazareth and on to Jerusalem with a cart laden with every good thing the community had to eat. We had lots of cushions and blankets and even a special bag with which to feed our donkey all the grain they were sending with us.

As the sun rose higher and higher and the day progressed, I could feel Mary becoming anxious to depart. With a squeeze of my hand in reassurance, we turned and waved and climbed into our cart. I noticed we now had more than one little donkey pulling our cart. We had two. I greeted them and they returned the greeting directly to my heart, and we embarked, holding the vibration of the living unity.

Holding the prayer to move beyond the confines of time, we traveled easily that day, making exceptional time. We took time to stop in the olive groves and to spread a blanket and eat, sharing an opulent picnic. We traveled along until the sun began to set, where, after much discussion, we decided to simply sleep out on the hillside because it was so beautiful in Nature. None of us wanted to be inside. So in the soft light of the setting sun, we pulled out our blankets and spent some time greeting the spirits of Nature. Once again we shared a feast of the things sent with us by the Essenes. Afterwards we sat sharing a comfortable silence.

As I sat beside my beloved and with my dearest friend, I looked out upon the rolling hills and saw the sheep dotting the hillside and a shepherd boy tending them. In my heart I knew that God, the living and endless Love, is ever that which shepherds us. I saw humanity as those sheep grazing, needing care. In my heart, I said, "Beloved Creator, I will be their shepherd in Your name, as Your Love, always." So was this analogy born. I am as the shepherd. Human hearts are what He/She tends. As I open as that living spirit, then I am one with the living God of Love and I am the shepherd of humanity.

So I was. And so I am, here to guide you, every one of you, as the Creator lives and breathes and loves, loves you as me, and loves me through you and the great circle of Love continues.

As our travels continued, I had many discussions with Judas and I could feel our friendship deepening. We had always loved and respected each other, and now I saw him as a strong and powerful man. It was with joy that we explored the things that moved our hearts with each other, and Mary honored us by giving us the space to do so. She would withdraw just a little way when we stopped to eat our meals if it seemed that Judas and I found this communion happening. She would sing songs of praise to the Goddess, or simply sit in meditation while we explored what moved us and deepened our connection as spiritual brothers.

I shared with Judas how my whole life is given to God — how every breath that I breathed, I breathed the Creator's name. I could see a movement in Judas, a deep recognition that in his heart he felt the same, and I was glad. I was moved and I was grateful. While the moments had not yet revealed a greater pattern, I sensed an expanding connection and that Judas had a part to play. For a moment or two I considered the idea of asking to be shown this greater unfolding, but then I chose to simply live in the present as I always did, allowing God to live through me as She would.

I also began to notice how Judas was looking at Mary. I saw in a flash what was happening, how her beauty moved him and made his heart remember the power of the Divine Feminine. Yet I could also see that he believed that this was Mary, not that it spoke of his own Twin Flame. In this moment, in a flash, I understood that Judas would have an important part to play in supporting my beloved when I was gone. I stopped in surprise and let that awareness settle.

I had always understood my transformation, for it had been within my being from the moment I was born, always with me in my consciousness. While many things were revealed in the moment, as the moments unfurled, the transformation of the body into the spirit for humanity had always been with me. I understood enough to know it was a symbol of the truth of the spirit within all of us. But at that point I knew no more.

Yet now I knew that what Judas felt for Mary, my beloved, would always be born of the deepest respect for me and for her. While it contained elements of excitement and passion, it was part of our pattern and so I accorded it. Once again I gave my Will to God, and my Love.

Traveling beyond the confines of time was quite an experience for Mary, for she kept trying to fit our travels back into the usual standards of measure. I kept showing her how to let go of the mind, how her mind was holding us on the old schedule and would make us late. I invited her to breathe, to remember how it feels to be the Light.

When she still held the tension and couldn't release the sense of urgency and worry, that night after Judas was deeply asleep, I took her hand and we walked out on a hillside. Finding an overhang where the rocks created a cave — for we were getting closer to Jerusalem and the landscape was changing — we took each other's hand and lay down on our blankets and pillows. Together we became the great union that had been honored by people for eons beyond time as the movement of the divine as masculine and feminine. We merged and became the music of the spheres. We became the Light once again.

We became the living circle of endless Love, exploding forth in a great orgasm of conscious life. In our spirits once again we accorded it and we acknowledged our timeless union. We became the great pillars of living Light and the heart that is always eternally giving. When at last we returned most of the way to our daily consciousness, I whispered into my beloved's ear, "Now, my heart, my Mary, you remembered. We are the Light. We are not the human." Snuggling against me, she moved her head in the affirmative and said, "Thank you, my Jeshua, for this remembrance."

Leap into the invisible realm
of all you cannot see
or know
and trust
the loving arms
that catch you there.

Chapter Seven

"Not one of us can ever be greater than any other."

As we made our way toward Jerusalem, Mary and I and Judas, I could still feel Mary's tension. I could feel unfamiliar waves of emotion radiating from her to me. It puzzled me at first but as I pondered it, I began to understand. I began to see that in this area, she was not trusting the greater vision, the truth of life — not trusting what I had shared from my deepest heart and open consciousness.

Instead she had been drawn into the limited view of the human personality — that little mind that continually spools forth the concept of time and creates a limited reality. Understanding this, I felt gratitude for that which she was showing me and a tenderness that moved me to reach out to her and to free her from these feelings that she might return to the living grace that is the eternal presence of Love. I knew that I needed to give to her unfailingly.

As we pulled into a wonderful clearing for the night, I spoke to Judas and told him that Mary needed me that evening and that having given her my heart, I was ever and always available to her. I asked him for understanding and to excuse me as I took her aside and spent the evening sharing my heart with her in order to bring us back into the perfect accord in which we lived.

Judas, being wise, smiled at me and agreed. "Don't worry about me, Jeshua. I am perfectly happy drinking in the evening sounds and contemplating all of this world we share with all the wonderful souls of humankind," he replied.

So it was that I said a prayer asking our Father/Mother/Creator on High to speak the truth of Love and Light through me to Mary. Giving again my will, my life, my being into God's keeping, I stepped from the stillness into the circle of her arms and took her gently aside into the shadows deepening beside the hill. Leading her to the top, we sat down, and began to speak.

Encircling her in my arms, I told her that so is my Love, ever and always encircling her forever, and that as we share our heartbeats, we share every moment's feeling. Thus, it was my deepest hope to share my Light with her and bring her back to joy.

Mary didn't speak but rather buried her head against my chest. Yet, I knew her so well, she might as well have spoken. I whispered my deepest truth which was that we were already joined by the living God. Our hearts and our union was sanctified in the living eternity of Light, and nothing in the world of men could ever interfere with this. Thus, if we never made it to a handfasting, it wouldn't matter, nor would it change my Love one bit, one single iota, for my heart and soul and being were forever hers.

As I spoke, I could feel her relax and I felt her resonance returning to the harmonious vibration of Love that we shared. Yet I knew she still held something in reserve for the tension hadn't completely left her. Allowing the living movement of Love to speak through my heart and voice, I lifted her chin and looked into her beloved eyes. Feeling the truth of her heart, I said to her, "My beloved. Place your hands upon my heart and listen." As she did so, my heart opened in a great rush and became a radiant sun, a splendor of awakening into the spirit. It brought us both together into the living hum that is the endless Light.

Holding my beloved close to me in spirit and in body, we were drawn by the magnetic presence of the living God and I whispered with the spirit's voice, "Look at our reality." As Mary and I opened into the truth of our spirit, a great living orb of Light became apparent, truly as radiant as the sun, shot through with gold and white and waves of Love, and ever singing the rhythm of the One. In this glorious orb of Light, the voice of Love spoke and said to her, "My daughter, you are endless. You are alive in every dimension, present in the hologram, filled with the truth of living Love I Am."

As we watched from the radiant center of our hearts, there shot forth in all directions living lines of possibilities in the eternal moment. Every one of them was a truth unfolding, life lived in the eternal Now. Each line of possibility was waiting for us to accord it, all of them pulsing at once and ready to be made manifest as the heart of the Creator we are together.

Into this orb of Light that reflected the Creator's inclusive reality, the spirit spoke a number of different things that had to do with our service on Earth, including our handfasting. Each one, the spirit said, "Do you accord this?" The moment we said, "Yes," like running lightning in a great tremor along lines of possibilities, the living voice of God said, "It is done."

As we watched, a shimmering rain of Light washed through our Twin Flame heart, bringing forth these possibilities. It made them manifest upon the Earth to become the fullness of life lived in the human reality. Every possibility blossomed at once, and into the space of our hearts, our beloved Creator spoke and said, "This is the truth of your beings. You are ever multi-dimensional and completely unlimited by any concept such as time. Only remember that you are the heart of the living Creator and all that you ordain shall come to pass, instantly if you will it, and effortlessly."

When the energy began to fade and we found ourselves once again on Earth sitting together in the velvet darkness, I could hear Mary's breath being drawn in and released as she absorbed this greater truth of our unlimited nature and gained the understanding of living beyond time in the eternal Now Moment of the spirit.

When the movement of God within me said, "She is ready," I opened my heart and voice and said to her, "Beloved, my precious Mary, we are this embodiment of Light and only if you choose, must you be limited by the perspective of the human mind and ego. So, shall we dance in the realms of Light, and as creators, ordain that to which the living spirit of Love says 'Yes'? Or shall we wait upon the world and walk a limited path, one foot before the other in something linear? I will abide by your will."

Though with human eyes I could not see her, in the spirit she was clear as day and the Light of Love and joy filled her countenance. Her smile, ever so sweet, touched my heart as always. She placed her arms around me and said, "Oh, Jeshua, I truly had no idea, although I had sensed this. Part of me knew I had allowed a limited view to take hold. But that part of me that sees itself as serving the human community sometimes can't help but be caught up in that way of doing things.

"Thank you for freeing me. I choose to live with you as the living Light of our Creator and to allow Love to speak that which is important into our hearts. Thus, I give my will again to the living and glorious Goddess and ask to be the embodiment of the truly Divine Feminine and to journey with you as a complete and living whole as we have been shown tonight."

I knew this was the truth of her heart. I knew also I had taken a chance in telling her I would abide with whatever she willed, because deep in my heart I knew I could not live the sub-creation. My buoyant nature could not be held down. And yet, she rose to my faith in her and opened up her heart again. Once again we were alive in the spirit. At the same time we were fully awake in the world and seeing everything as God's face.

After a time of silence, filled with the rhythm of our hearts, I said to her, "My beloved, what would please you? How much time would you like to prepare for our handfasting? When would you like to arrive at the Jerusalem desert community of the Essenes?"

As she held me even tighter, she said, "I only need a few days but I wanted to be able to attune to the group and find harmony and to prepare myself to be your bride as a symbol for those who see the Light by which we are choosing always to live." With a kiss, I said, "So be it." Holding her had opened my heart, and in an instant we ordained that reality and felt it begin to manifest from the living spirit into the world. We heard the voice of our Creator say within us, "It is done."

"Now what do we do?" she asked. "How do we make a journey in two days that should normally take us two weeks?" With Love, I said, "Dearest Mary, it is easy. We just travel the path before us in perfect faith that time does not exist in the realms of Love. We will arrive exactly when we have chosen, regardless of the evidence before our eyes. Our physical eyes are the eyes that see duality — that see a world of past and future, of linear time. But as we live as the heart of God, we live beyond this illusion, and as the Creator's Love, we make manifest that which is our perfection in movement."

And so we returned to our campsite to find that Judas had prepared a fire and was cooking a wonderful meal which he had manifested in some way that he seemed to consider a secret and a gift to us. With our hearts content, we shared our dinner. Watching the crackling fire, our hearts danced and we became a living flame of worship. Without a word being spoken, the three of us moved into harmony. I knew that Judas was aligned with us and that he could see the truth of the spirit and feel the Love.

I clasped their hands again, my beloved and my brother, and once again the voice of Love spoke through me and said, "Though the way may be difficult when seen through human eyes, that which we are here to do is truly exalted. We shall do it always in Love, regardless of the view of others, knowing in our hearts, we are the outreach of The One and that which is enacted on the world stage is always the Creator's gift through us to humanity."

Judas bowed his head and said, "I give my life to you — to you, Jeshua and Mary, to you, God. I give you all I am. I give my will and my heart, my consciousness, my very breath, my body, and I ask, oh, glorious Creator, that you would use me in support of this mission, always. I am your humble servant and the servant of Jeshua as he shines as this glorious heart with his Mary. I am grateful." The movement of his Love was truly palpable and we sat together, feeling the presence and the living vibration, the River of Life moving through us and joining us together perfectly in the deepest Love and dedication.

So our travels took us effortlessly and perfectly around the city of Jerusalem, over the hills and into the desert, where on the east side of the mountains in a warren of caves extending eastward over the desert was the community of the Essenes — those who lived in seclusion and those who spent part of their time serving in the city of Jerusalem.

As we came up to the entrance, suddenly there was great commotion. I recognized the vibration of Micah, the leader of this community and my dear lifetime friend who carried the energy on Earth for Archangel Michael, and whose spirit was as a living sword cutting through to the truth in every situation, always in humility. I found myself excited just as I was as a boy. When we would return from our travels and head toward home, always we stopped in this community and then at the Temples in Jerusalem.

Whether I was a very young child with Joseph and Mary or whether I was returning with a caravan as a young man full of new learning, I always came and sat at the feet of Micah and learned.

Running, we met each other and grabbed each other in a deep hug. Though I was a large man, I felt Micah lifting me, which came as a surprise because he was not very large or strong. I knew it must be the joy of the spirit within him. He stood there in his robe and sandaled feet, his hair the color of the sand but streaked now with lines of gray and white. He had a face that was always serene and that anyone would call handsome. His eyes smiled from the depth of his being and twinkled. Their gray color sparkled and reflected the sky. I could feel his consciousness expanding, and still we hugged.

Finally I pulled away and said, "Micah. This is Mary. Mary who is the Magdalene. You might know of her. This is Mary who is also my beloved, my Twin Flame, my own heart. We have come because the spirit moved us to be joined here. We come to ask if you are willing to do this?"

With a laugh, he threw back his head and said, "Oh, Jeshua, of course I am. In fact, I have been calling you to come here for I knew — you know how news travels — that you and Mary were now together, and I knew from the living spirit that you were to be joined here. So welcome! Welcome! Come in. I am honored to perform your handfasting, to join you in the spirit of the endless living One, and to share you with this community."

As we walked up the walk that had been made out of the sand and rocks, he explained to me that everyone here knew of me and of that which I am as the living heart of Christ — that which they called the Messiah, come to the world. As he spoke, I knew immediately that I would have a challenge to make them understand that it was not "me," the person of Jeshua who had come to be a savior. Rather, it was simply my heart as a living conduit for that glorious and endless Love of the Creator who lives and has His/Her being in all of us, simply waiting for the veil to be lifted and the truth to be set free.

Turning and taking my beloved's hand, we entered the doorway to find many changes and improvements over the years. The greatest one was brand new windows everywhere. The breeze flowed perfectly between them. There were many additions made of both rock and wood. From the window I could see a network of meandering walkways and I felt both the excitement and the peace of this community. I also felt its purity. All energies here pointed to the living God. For this I said a prayer of gratitude.

Before we knew it, we were standing in the community room, a very large room, open and airy, in which they took their meals and shared as a community. There were many comfortable chairs and long tables. We were surrounded with men and women and with children who greeted us with exuberance, joy and genuine welcome. I was content. I could see that Mary was ecstatic for the harmony was instant among us. The moment Micah announced that we would be handfasted in three days, a roar of acceptance and joy moved through everyone, and we were instantly surrounded with their best wishes and their excitement in getting to witness and to share in this occasion.

Yet I also felt an undercurrent of worship, even idolatry, that was holding me, Jeshua, up as something grand. I knew that I would speak to them, allowing the spirit to create the words and to be for them the living mirror of God, to show them their own beauty, their truth as the living Christ, as the heart of God sharing the unified heartbeat. I knew that they would understand and would open themselves to the truth that lived within, and I was grateful.

The next few days passed in a flurry of activity, and while I longed to have some time with my dear friend, Micah, it seemed I had not a moment. But Mary was in ecstasy, and this was enough for me. I was filled with gladness and simply watched in joy as she delighted in the preparations, in having all the women rushing around doing her bidding and helping her to feel beautiful in brand new and exciting ways. Of course, to me, she was stunning in every way — the living sunlight of my spirit, my bread, my meat, my wine, the candle of my life, my heart. But still, something in her wanted to experience this time and to share this sweetness with these women and this community.

I, too, took delight in all the preparations, even letting the women create new clothes for me, and basked in this joyous community of Love. Each morning we gathered for prayers and then sat silently in meditation. As we sat, I could feel our spirits joining and creating a brand new tapestry of a living heart of service, waiting to be held up to the world as a new way of living in perfect harmony and community.

I knew that ultimately this would occur, because these people were weaving a pattern, just as Mary and I were weaving one also. We relished each moment, coming together only at night, but our nights were filled with joy, with bliss and with the excitement of anticipation for the special time when we would make our vows before them, this community of the brothers and sisters of my heart.

It came to pass that the night before our handfasting, the whole community gathered to honor us with special food which for them was no little thing, for they tended to eat very simply. This night we had many courses and we even had dessert. All of them were truly enjoying the evening. After the meal was finished and everything cleared away, I rose and began to speak. First I thanked them with all my heart for welcoming us so completely and for being my brothers and sisters in spirit. As I spoke I looked at Judas and our hearts connected. I sent him a message of how much I cherished him as my brother, beyond all reckoning.

Then I continued to speak, asking the spirit to speak as me. I told them that it was not Jeshua that they should be worshiping but that only the living God should ever be the focus of the worship of the human heart and being. "Therefore," I said, "I point you ever and always to Him/Her, to our glorious cosmic parents, to the living unity in which we move, breathe, have our being and sing the songs of life."

I spoke about religion. I said, "There will be a tendency to make a religion of the things that happen through Mary and me, through all of us as sisters and brothers in this new pattern of awakening for humankind. In truth, there is only one religion and it is the religion of the living God, originating in God, flowing out from Him/Her and containing everything.

"It wraps All That Is in Her Love and gives us the power to recognize God's presence in everything, including in us, but certainly not exclusively. This will never be in one of us more than any other, for we are all born of the Light. We live in the endless Love. Our consciousness is one shared consciousness of our Creator. Not one of us can ever be greater than any other. Anything else is ever and always only delusion.

"So when you look at me and you know that I have come to be the life and Light, to be the embodiment of the Christos, know that I am the mirror for your own heart and consciousness — that Mary and I are the examples of Real Love, the truth of the Creator's heart made manifest, purely and simply, as the vehicle of bringing God's Love to Earth. This is your truth as well, and I accord it in every one of you. I rejoice in the Creator's presence as it stands before me, wearing your face, sharing your movements and loving perfectly with your heart, the heart of the Christ."

There was complete silence when I stopped speaking. Yet, I could feel the vibration had completely changed and I felt a living harmony moving among us like a shared breath. I knew that they had understood me perfectly, according all that I shared with their hearts and accepting it. From that moment on, there was a deep amazing unity in that community and all of us functioned as one being. Our consciousness had opened to each other perfectly. Our thoughts were shared instantly and fully. The Love we had flowing among us was filled with the radiant presence of our Creator, nourishing us through each other and directly with every breath.

This community of Essenes, on the edge of the desert, had suddenly become a great Light for the world. The oasis of our Love brought the desert to life, literally. Things began to grow and flourish, and the community which had struggled with a garden because of the heat, saw great changes. Suddenly they found the garden rich, green and growing. When they came to me and asked, I said, "Everything is possible with God." And so it is.

When love surrounds us
drawing us close
and we feel the soft breath of intimacy
and the rhythmic caress
of an unseen heart
we are home.

Chapter Eight

"This understanding will be the thing that brings your greatest gift to humanity..."

As Mary became happily involved in all the preparations for our joining, I felt called into a soul communion with Micah, and I knew that he would share with me something very important. I drew him aside and spoke to him and he agreed, for he felt the same reminder of our powerful communion with each other and with the great starry, open cosmos of the Beloved who is our Creator. Micah and I were both open to the glorious communion with all life which is the inheritance of every one of us.

With him, I could speak of the things dearest to my heart. Not only did he understand. He shared the experience. This for me was the greatest gift. The only other people with whom I had shared in such a way were my beautiful and precious parents. While I shared intimately with Mary, my beloved, it was different and I was realizing the depth of this difference as we had traveled toward Jerusalem. I spoke of this to Micah and I shared with him what I was seeing, and he listened. He accorded my truth and shared my heart.

I shared with him the depth of my Love for Mary. I also explained my latest understanding — that Mary sees the world very differently from me. I told him that I had looked through Mary's eyes and was astounded. To me the world was made of patterns of Light and the deep and powerful web of continual communion with the dancing presence always of the Creator's Love. The Love that God is was ever being multiplied, extended and gifted to every being.

But when I looked at the world through Mary's eyes, I saw a world drenched in color, rich with the nuances of a physical life that was not part of my reality. I also came to understand some other things as I glanced at a world so different from mine. I understood not only the nuances of being feminine but I understood some new things about being human, for Mary had the gift of being immersed in the world of humanity as a counterpoint, a grounding for me. Through her eyes, I began to realize that this world, so rich, vibrant and intense, was based on a completely different foundation and was essentially a trick of the ego, powerful in its ability to present to the consciousness of humankind a belief that the world was powerful and not God.

When I had seen this, I was shocked, stunned, for I had never considered such a view of life. I was always immersed in the Creator's Love, dancing in the living and glorious waves of joy, and ever and always focused on God as the power, the center of the universe and as the grace that gives us the gift of life. Because of my orientation, all things were provided for me. Every heartbeat was a heartbeat of plenty and the communion with all life made it simple to call forth the energies and to manifest anything that was needed.

Yet my glimpse of the world through Mary's eyes brought a complete shift in my consciousness concerning the bereft heart of humankind that had lost that deep assurance of God's place in their universe. As I spoke, Micah reached out and took my hand. We sat knee to knee and communed together and he said to me, "Jeshua. I have seen many things about your life, about your Love and about this pattern. I know by the grace of the Creator's Love that you will come to understand this difference, and that this understanding will be the thing that brings your greatest gift to humanity."

As he spoke, the Heavens opened and rained life, and the vibration of the presence of the One moved into my being with a powerful message. That message confirmed what Micah had said — that I was to understand this experience that formed the perspective of humanity. When I did, it would be the bridge that Love built back to God. I bowed my head and tears formed in my eyes, and a great feeling of honor and of Love moved through me. I whispered in my heart of hearts, "I am here, God. Make of me a vehicle for humanity's return to you."

Yet, even though these things had come from spirit and the voice of Love spoke them in my heart, I still was stunned by this realization of humanity placing their focus outside their heart and away from God. I knew that I must walk in trust and in the Creator's Love and live every step in faith, knowing that Love's Will would be revealed to me as every moment called it forth through need, and that I had no need to reach for understanding that would only come when I was ready to find it.

I trusted God, My Divine Father and My Mother, absolutely, totally, completely, and I knew that as I lived and breathed in my devotion, then everything would come to me in the living present with the blessing of that wonderful unfolding that God gives us. Each moment is sufficient unto itself, and perfect. I said this to Micah. I spoke my faith, and yet I knew that my consciousness had been altered. Something new had been planted within me, and with it, an even deeper desire to help, to assist these precious hearts to return to the glorious Love in which I lived. Love surrounded me palpably and filled my life with grace and lifted me into the pure joy of merging with every movement of life as it expressed itself as the Creator playfully exploring All That Is.

As preparations moved forward for my joining with Mary, the days were filled with new learning and expansion, and drenched in Light and anticipation of the affirmation of our Twin Flame heart, as we declared our dedication to the living, breathing harmony of God. As the time neared, I began to be excited, for I felt the presence of the Angels gathering. In my heart I placed a call for my beloved parents, my guardians of my Earth life, Mary and Joseph, for I deeply desired to have them present to witness this ceremony of my heart.

The day before our handfasting dawned bright, though chilly, and I felt the balancing of the energies symbolized by that returning of daylight and darkness to the perfect expression of harmony and equality that is the Equinox. I felt the Love for my beloved rise in my heart. I also felt the deepening of our communion and of the fires of our transcendent passion. Yet I did not go to her for I felt that a sacred space was being built within us that I honored by keeping my inner silence and lifting ever higher in the Light, that I might truly be the living conduit of the Creator's Love.

That afternoon as I returned from that deeper silence, I began to recognize new energies in the compound and instantly I knew that my parents had arrived. I was joyous and rushed outside to greet them. Taking them into the chamber that had been assigned to me, I wrapped them each in a hug and gazed into their eyes and thanked them profusely for hearing and responding to my message.

My mother laughed and said, "Jeshua, we wouldn't miss this.." I asked, "How did you travel? Was it difficult?" My mother gave me her secret smile and said, "Oh, no, it was easy. We simply willed it and it occurred." I laughed with her. I said, "I have not yet taught this to my beloved and so we traveled in more conventional ways." Then Joseph spoke and said, "We already know this, for Jeshua, we follow you. We follow you in our communion with the Creator that links all of us together always. Thus we always know how you are doing and where you are."

"I am so glad," I responded. "I love knowing this. Let us make a deep commitment here and now to stay in touch, no matter how great the distance and no matter what God asks of us." We made that pact. We spoke of deep and often unknown things, arcane knowledge, if you would, and we spoke of the pattern that we were building and how this public union tied into it. My mother said, "This is important, your handfasting, and your honoring of the Essenes who have held the Light and prepared the way for you for so long, who have lived in purity and have spent their time and their hearts in dedication to the living Christ and to the awakening of the world.

"But I am feeling, my Jeshua, my son, that there is meant to be something else, something that will speak to the population, that will speak to all of the people about Love and about the power of commitment and dedication, the power and the beauty of the joined heart and the sacred reality of Twin Flame Love." The moment she spoke these things, my heart accorded it. I knew that she was right.

I also knew that that was a revelation for another day. Right now, this was the moment, this moment of crystalline purity with my parents, and the preparation for tomorrow's joining with my Mary, the Magdalene, who held within her womanhood the feminine energy of humankind. It was she who brought from the Earth through her heart, in its dedication, the outreach of the Earth for the Creator's Love — the fire in human hearts to be free and the power of the feminine and its yearning to understand itself as divine.

I saw this as I spent this evening in preparation for our joining, the wedding of our hearts into one. Once again I understood that both things were true. We held a very different energy as the masculine and the feminine and yet, we shared the one Creator's Love and made it manifest through us. In that time as I prepared for sleep, the Light filled my consciousness and I knew in a richer, deeper way than ever before that the Creator is easily all things and that in Him/Her there are no opposites. There is only the blending that creates movement. Thus did I understand the masculine and feminine ever more clearly as the movement of God and the Creator's revelation of Herself to us and to Himself.

I took my rest, content in the Creator's Love, suspended in that endless support, linked with my beloved with every breath and drinking my fill of the Light that always provides for us. While I did partake of traditional repast with my friends and with those with whom I shared on my travels, in truth I lived easily by drinking the Light and absorbing the Love. I knew that the living unity was my nourishment. That nourishment supported my heart, the heart that is the center of our identity in our relationship with God.

Because our handfasting was arriving, I was in a deeply introspective place, introspection that took me into my heart and through my heart, to the One who is all things to us, including the focus of our devotion, our identity and our joy. Thus I spent the night preparing myself for my beloved, opening to my part as the living embodiment of the Divine Masculine and a new choice for giving — to give my heart, my spirit, all that I am, to the one whom God created with me as my counterpart, as my heart and as the feminine which showed me the truth of Love in ever new ways.

The morning came. The sun rose and the dawning of Yule brought the day, not only of the celebration of the patterns of Light, the turning of the Earth that is the Equinox, but also my glorious union with my true Love.

When I give myself to love,
I see through love's eyes,
speak with love's lips,
touch with love's fingers,
taste with love's tongue,
and hear with love's ears.

Chapter Nine

"His spirit is with me and he is waiting."

[NOTES FROM YAEL: Mary Magdalene was with me from the moment that I awoke today, and she is showing me how she looked in the time of Jesus. I can feel not only her presence spiritually but see her standing before me physically. She is so exceptionally clear, so "real" right here with me that I would like to describe her to you.

She is beautiful and radiant. She has long red hair that is fairly wavy and falls almost to her waist. It's red but it's not a deep dark red. It is definitely red with gold in it. Though for some reason I always pictured her with lots of curly hair, her hair is actually fairly soft and fine and looks like red-gold sunlight washing over her body.

Her eyes are green and they are twinkling. She has a smile that just lights up her face. Her skin is very pale and she has freckles and she is voluptuous. I would guess she is about 5'6" and very curvy, very womanly in her figure and very present on the Earth. You can feel that she is grounded. I can tell that where her sandals rest upon the Earth, she is feeling that contact. She is so alive and vibrant and the Earth is very real to her as a living breathing being. I can hear her laughter.

She is wearing a dress that we would probably call a robe. It is very simple in its design. It falls over her hips and down into the dust of the Earth. It's white and it looks like *linen. You can see the weave in it. It has a blue piece along the hem, a medium to dark blue. Around her shoulders is a shawl more tightly woven and a little thicker fabric, but it is not wool. It also is white with the blue edges. I get the feeling that this is her trademark, the colors she most likes to wear. She is saying that she sends her greetings to all of humanity.]*

Mary Magdalene speaks:

At last it was the day of my joining with my beloved, my Jeshua. I woke in the morning and I shot out of bed and did a dance around my room. I waved my arms up to the sky and stomped my feet upon the Earth. I said, "Goddess, I am ready. Let me be the glorious expression of You, this day, as I wed my heart, my Jeshua. Oh, I am ready."

Filled with delight, anticipation and almost unbearable excitement, I quickly looked for my sisters in the community who joined me in laughter. We began the day with a wonderful, completely uplifting, ritual celebrating the turning of the seasons, celebrating the return of the Light and celebrating the glorious dance of Love that is the greatest gift in a life on Earth.

We sang songs in our women's voices to the Goddess and to her Love and to all the ways that she moves through the feminine to bless the world. We sang songs of the rising of the Light within us. We affirmed ourselves as keepers of the flame. I felt myself as a fire burning with passion and devotion to Jeshua and burning with dedication to serving the children of Love, every heart that blesses the world simply by its presence.

I reaffirmed my commitment to the Temple, to that deeply powerful path for women, while at the same time I spoke of my certainty that life with Jeshua was already changing my perspective. I welcomed this, giving myself once again to the living spirit that She might do her Will through me, especially this day. Then, as do brides everywhere, I began to decorate myself and to decorate the Temple in a flurry of joyous activity. We rushed about creating a tableau of mystical remembrance with light and incense, with paintings and drawings that we all brought forth, and colorful cloth that we strung up around the Temple and draped over many cushions.

We wove braids of grasses and herbs to tie around the pillows in the Temple. The room in which our handfasting was to occur was the main room of Essene worship, carved out of the mountain itself like a womb, like the Mother. It had not a window anywhere, just the feeling of being embraced by the living intelligence born into the very rock that marked for us the turning of the Ages and spoke of immortality. The rocks always spoke to me and I acknowledged them. They taught me so many things about remaining steadfast in the observance of the turning of the Earth and the seasons.

As I stood in the Temple on that morning, I acknowledged all of our allies in Nature — the blessed Earth and her intelligence; the powerful time of winter; the turning of the seasons of our lives, just like the turning of each year. Most of all, I celebrated the gift of this great Love that I had never even imagined, and I was exuberant.

All the women of this community of Essenes were there with me and for me this day. Each one brought forth her special gift and honored me with it. They brought to me many things — special foods for Jeshua and me to share later; tapestries that they had woven with their hands; clothing they had made; statues of the glorious Divine Feminine, and honored my spirit with them. I began to feel so cherished, so honored and so grateful for the glorious sisterhood that connected women everywhere.

As the day went on, it was time for me to get ready and I was taken to a special chamber for brides that was filled with things that represented the feminine and the power of the Goddess. The Essenes accorded all paths to The One, and so there were things in that room from many religions. There were statuaries from India that showed the *lingam* and the *yoni*. There were drawings of Love-Making. There were those things universally appealing to women — for my hair and for my body.

I allowed my sisters to assist me to become the bride that is the symbol of the Goddess' glory as She moves forth to mate with Her counterpart, with God. They brought me water warmed outside over the fire and helped me bathe and wash my hair. They braided my hair with colorful yarns and ribbons and painted my face with sparkles. I had never been one to adorn myself with cosmetics but I couldn't resist on this day. One of the women who was young and very beautiful appeared with her precious cache of makeup — kohl from East India and malachite ground very finely for the eyes, to set off my green eyes, she said. I laughed but I accepted, along with a pot of rouge for my face made of special clay. I made myself ready for the joining.

To my robe that fell in drapes around me, I was given the addition of a golden girdle with chains of gold that hung down to my knees. I thought it was very beautiful. Around my neck I placed the Goddess symbol beneath my robe next to my heart. I held my hand over it and said a prayer, asking to be Her pure vessel. Then I adorned my head with the most beautiful scarf. I had never seen anything like it. It had actual threads of gold woven into it, with all the colors of the rainbow. This I placed around my head, tied and draped, that it cascaded with my hair down to my waist. I was ready.

"Oh, no, you are not ready," said my beautiful friend who had brought forth her cache before. She rushed out of the room and came back holding the most beautiful pair of shoes I had ever seen. "What are these?" I asked. "Ah, they are also from India," she said. "Aren't they beautiful?" I just stared. Like the threads in my scarf, the girdle around my waist, they appeared to be made of gold. The toes of the shoes came forward and curled up just a little at the front. I thought, "These are shoes made for dancing......" Then I said, "I can't wear these. They probably wouldn't even fit my feet." She said, "Watch!" Getting down on her knees, she put them on and they fit perfectly.

I just had to dance, so I danced all around the room, throwing back my head, reaching out with my heart, feeling the delicious rush of life, the touch of Nature, the movement of the world — hearing all of it at once. As quickly as my dance had begun, it stopped, for I allowed life to flow through me, always living perfectly in the moment. Truly, I lived in joy. Thus I felt the energy change, very definitely and completely.

Suddenly standing in that chamber with women all around me, I felt my Jeshua. I felt him as clearly as if he were standing before me in his body. I felt his heart touch mine. I felt the silence of his being extending to me. We held that moment together. When I looked up at all the faces around me who were wondering what was happening, I said in a whisper, "Jeshua is here. His spirit is with me and he is waiting. It is time."

In a living cloud of white and sparkling beauty surrounded by the feminine in the form of my sisters of spirit, I walked very carefully in my golden feet through the compound to the Temple — through the hallways carved in the stone that stood as sentinels of time. As I walked, the whole pathway was filled with lamps burning. I followed this path of Light to my Jeshua, just as the sun was setting. I knew in my heart that when I spoke, the words would fall from my lips as nectar from the living Goddess. I knew that when we kissed, something majestic would appear in the world that had never been present before.

Thus, with eyes shining with tears of joy, I stopped at the entrance to the Temple. I looked around that great room carved in stone with pillars in four corners. All around were those whom Jeshua called "his community," those whose hearts embraced me also. Before me on the other side of the room stood my Jeshua. Before him was the altar upon which burned the flame to The Living One, the one life of which we are made, the flame that was always lit both here in the community of the Essenes and a similar flame lit in the Temple in Jerusalem.

I breathed in the scent of the incense and the wonderful fragrance of my Jeshua who in being and body was like the Lotus of God that I would recognize anywhere. Though we had discussed and rehearsed this ritual, I stood rooted to that spot — me, Mary who always was filled with action, delight, always gregarious, out-spoken. I was mute, held in the breath of eternity.

All around the room, the vast room of stone that had held so many ceremonies of worship — its very walls were filled with a reverberation of joy and devotion — all around it were lamps burning as symbols of the coming Light. I realized that this Light was Jeshua. Then I realized that it was also me, for he and I are one being, and that stopped me for a moment. When I looked up again, our eyes met across the room and the silence was so complete you couldn't even hear the people breathing. I could feel all the hearts of this community rejoicing, even in the stillness.

I looked into those eyes that I knew so well, that countenance so handsome. His hair was like spun gold dancing in the lamplight. As I watched, he began to smile. That smile reached in and took my heart and lifted it to the pinnacle of joy, and I moved to that smile, step-by-step. The women parted and went around us, creating a circle of the Mother's Love, and surrounding them was a circle of men. In the middle of these circles was the altar, behind which was Jeshua. Beside him was Micah.

As I neared the altar, I sank to my knees and offered my prayers to the Goddess. Jeshua sank to his knees and began his prayer to The One God of Love. From the four corners voices began to speak, greeting the elements, acknowledging the turning of the year. More voices began to speak from within the circle — first a man and then a woman. They spoke from the holy scriptures of every religion, all saying the same thing, every one affirming the Creator's Love — that we are that Love made manifest and asking us to hold fast to these things and the spirit and truth as the heart of our union. To this, I gave my "Yes" and so did Jeshua.

More voices, more speaking, more scripture was recited, and then, the priestess rose and came to the altar. She raised her arms and invoked the Divine Feminine and brought Her joy and His wisdom into us, asking that we be granted the true fertility, the fertility of giving birth to perfect Love for each other and in service.

When the celebration of Yule had been proclaimed, Micah stood forth and began to speak. In a voice that was deep and resonant he called out the names of the Creator in every language, honoring every element of humankind, every doorway of worship, every path to Love. Then, he began our ceremony. He spoke of the merging of heart and spirit and consciousness. He spoke of being the womb of Creation itself. He spoke of the trust both given and received in a handfasting. And he spoke of our choice, our choice to be renewed each Yule, to continue this union, this commitment. This is a part of every ceremony of handfasting, even to your day.

Then he called us to come together. We walked around the altar and stood before Micah. We spoke the words that he gave us. Then we spoke out of the movement of Love in our own hearts and gave each other our whole being — heart, soul, body, consciousness, eternity, all of it. We promised to be for the world that Light.

When we were done, Micah called for everyone present to be our witness. Then he took our hands and joined them and tied them with another rope of gold. Again, I was surprised at the opulence. Then Micah spoke and gave the reasons for this rope of gold. He said that we were honored by all of them as that which would bring humanity out of the sea of darkness and into the Light of our Creator — into the Light of the eternal day that never ends and the Love that is all-encompassing. He said that we were the living gold of the spirit and he honored us deeply. Then he braided that rope around our wrists and created out of it a ribbon that hung down between us.

Filled with awe, washed in devotion, completely inspired and totally in Love, I leaned forward for the kiss. When our lips met, my being was flooded with Jeshua, with the taste of him, with the touch, with the spirit, with the Light, with the beating of his heart that I could feel within mine. I realized even our hearts had been part of this joining. Though we had been joined completely in the spirit, we were bringing this joining into the world, palpably, with this ritual.

Thus we stood, awash in Love, filled with the Creator's Light. The room was full of dancing flames of gold from all the lamps. We breathed in each other and became that one heart in a way that was new and powerful. Micah held the silence for us and the whole community followed suit, joining in meditation. I could hear the songs of the Angels and their trumpeting the message of our union throughout the Heavens. Jeshua later confirmed this, for he experienced it, too.

After the silence had filled our beings, we began to feel the sweet spirit of this community, the purity of all the hearts within it, their dedication to Jeshua and thus, to me, and their willingness to support our lives and message with all they were. These things I could read in the auras in the room. They touched me deeply and I was amazed.

I had truly believed that only in the Goddess Temple would I feel such accord with a group. I had thought it was because the Goddess Temple was a temple of women. In that moment I realized it was the unity that was the deepest truth of the living spirit, and totally beyond gender. Here in this Temple, joined with my beloved, I had found the community of heart and spirit that was to become for me a great vehicle of learning, especially learning more about the world and the spirituality of all its people, not just those who celebrate the Goddess or God but those who celebrate in any way the living spirit in all of us.

In those moments, at the end of our ritual, what I felt was the sense of community that was so solid that it was irresistible. It felt truly like coming Home in a new way, a way that spoke to the expansion of my spirit that had come with Jeshua, with his presence in my life. I had begun to understand the place of the Divine Masculine in a whole new way, as totally synchronous and complete equal with the Feminine. In this realization I could sense the voice of the spirit that speaks within our being, saying "Yes" and whispering to my heart that this was part of my mission. I was to hold forth the truth of Real Love and true equality — equality of heart and spirit, rather than body and our shared place at the center of all as creators.

The ceremony was finished and we were being embraced, first by Micah and then by the priestess.

Then everyone was crowding around us with congratulations. Everyone wanted to hug us. Soon, laughing, Jeshua and I put our arms around each other's waist, and opened our other arms, welcoming all of them. After countless hugs and sincerest wishes for the greatest joy together, we all began to move toward the feast and into an evening of pure fun and celebration with lots of dancing, and music and singing. Everyone who played an instrument played for us.

As the evening began to calm down, people began to speak their heart's truth about Jeshua, about all that he brought to Earth. Many spoke of me also and what it meant to them to see this Love and know its purpose, totally dedicated to service. I was so moved that I could not speak. I could not gather myself enough to make a response. I was overwhelmed by the beauty of these hearts and their sincerity. The evening progressed from dancing and singing to the singing of prayers and songs of gratitude.

While the singing continued, I looked at my beloved, my Jeshua, and he was looking at me with a silent message in his eyes. I heard it very clearly. I reached down and took his hand and we began to make our way to our special chamber that had been given to us, decorated and blessed for our personal celebration. I, for one, intended to take advantage of this!

Love is such a perfect lover,
caressing and coaxing our souls
to blossom
from seeds hidden deep
within the soul.

Chapter Ten

"We were blissful in our Love... lifted, transported..."

Jeshua speaks:

We stayed in the Essene community outside Jerusalem where we laughed and danced and worked and loved all through that winter and into the spring, waiting for the Creator to move us. The Essenes gathered us in and nurtured us with their Love. Their days were spent doing the tasks that living takes, but with such Love and serenity that it was truly a spiritual experience just being amongst them.

We taught. We spoke with the voice of the living spirit of Love as it moved through our hearts and our vocal chords in blessing. The Essene community knew of our mission and understood the forces of life, as well as the movement of the seasons. In that community the old and the new were merging, and a greater truth was being born in their wisdom.

It was a joy to share the energies and the Light and all that we were being shown, and to have it accepted and reflected back to us so enthusiastically. Micah and the elders in the Essene community had deep and expansive wisdom. As they sat with us and looked at the Heavens, we spoke of the messages that we had received and that they had received about us.

Together we gained a deeper view of our lives and of the service upon which we now embarked.

We saw what we had always known — that we would have a limited time together. We knew that we must live every moment to the fullest, with the most open hearts, and that we must cherish each moment with each other as if it were our very last. We made this promise to each other when we said our vows on the Equinox, and we kept that vow to each other until the end.

At night, Mary and I would sit beyond the community's gates up on a plateau under the stars, and we would be blanketed by God's Love and held in the arms of the Mother. Our Love continued to grow and blossom gloriously from the moment that we spoke our heartfelt vows. The essence of God's richness and Love sparked and grew into great flames of ecstasy in any moment that we so much as touched. Our force fields would simply come together and we were blissful in our Love, lifted, transported in our unity. We walked in a world of pure Light and endless beauty.

During the day sometimes we would stroll through the community's gardens. Other times we would hike out into the rocky hills. Everywhere we went, we were greeted by the Nature Spirits and the Devas, by every form of life, for they knew that we were weaving a new pattern into the world. As the revelations came to us fast and furious, Mary and I began to get the whole picture and to truly understand what Nature already knew — that we were here on Earth to literally weave a New World, strand of Light by strand of Light, intention by intention in Love, completely in tune with the Creation in every second and moved by God with every step.

The Web of Light and beauty that we were creating through our Love was to supplant the dualistic sub-creation. That Web of Light is now coming to fruition here in you. We saw, with the vision God gave us, the arc of our lives and of our service and that our lives were dedicated to you, you who now hear my voice. Everything we did, we did in Love, holding you in our vision and our hearts. While some of you were actually present and embodied there in that life in the Holy Land, many of you were all around us in the spirit and we easily communed with you.

We saw that this new weaving of Light that began there in us had to hold strong in order to anchor the future, a future centered in God. We also saw what we would be holding when it came time for the seeming end of that mission. We knew that the Web of Light, the Net of God, the substance of the New World must be held by us so perfectly that even those events that were coming could not dislodge it at all.

Many of you speak now of the Christ Grid. It was begun in that life in us. We consciously used the power of our Love-Making to create those strands of Light and to allow the Creator's Love to flow through us with such potency that we could weave the Light through all the tangled webs of the sub-creation and the ego mind's ball of thought.

It was during those days in the Essene community that we more and more clearly saw the vision and began the steps. We also found that we were instructed by all the Masters who walked with us in those nights full of stars. All were divine partnerships. Each pair of Divine Masculine and Divine Feminine explained to us in those magical nights how it was and what it meant to come together as the movement of God, as the power of Creation itself.

As the spring came, something in our hearts said, "I Am calling." When we sat and listened or went forth and walked up into the rocks, out into the sand, we found that the call remained steady and pointed us East and South. However, before beginning any new journey, we wanted to travel to Nazareth again to speak with Mary and Joseph and share with them that to which we felt we were being called.

As the spring came to Judea and the light rose over Jerusalem, we put on our heaviest sandals and wrapped ourselves in robes and cloaks and journeyed out. We said our farewells to the Essenes and to our respective Temples, and we walked along the dusty paths of Judea through Samaria and into Galilee. Our homecoming was so sweet and Mary already felt like she was one with my family. We felt the need for the clarity of my mother and of Joseph, for we knew that they could verify that which we received as our message and the beginning of our mission.

Home in Nazareth again, it was a delight to be gathered with my family. As we sat on the front stoop together, some of us in chairs that Joseph had made, we watched the children playing in the streets, laughing and jouncing. We knew such a sweet contentment as the Light slanted across the adobe brick, and everything was burnished with that sweet spring sunlight.

As I stared at my sandaled feet, I realized how many steps I was about to take. I felt strong in my spirit and in my body that I knew was made of Light, and I felt so deeply grateful in my heart for my beloved, my precious Mary, the Magdalene. I knew what a gift that God has given, that each of us might know our heart so readily by seeing it before us in our Twin Flame — that we might know that although we are one heartbeat, we are truly two streams of energy. Just as the physical heart is the life blood of the body, so are we the life blood of the spirit.

Mary, my mother, took a moment for prayer, turning herself deep within. Her countenance was so beautiful, her face like alabaster, her hair shining in the sun and falling out beyond her headpiece, the drape of fabric that she always wore. I marveled at her purity and beauty, and I felt honored — honored to know that I was part of her and that she had ushered me into the world. I was deeply grateful that she and Joseph could hold the harmonics so perfectly that I could come into being without the birth canal and be fully the living spirit in the world.

Spontaneously I reached over in blessing and placed one hand on each of their foreheads. Mary's eyes opened instantly wide and said, "Oh, my son, you are truly blessed. You are the Light of The One blazing, blazing forth now for the world." So I said, "Dearest mother, what are you seeing? Is it time now for us to leave and are we going South and East out of Judea? Tell me what you see."

She said many words to us then, all of which fell from her mouth like blessings — words of God's spirit falling on our eager hearts and ears. Mary and I clasped hands, my beautiful Magdalene, my goddess, and the excitement rose in our hearts because we knew it was beginning. Mary, my mother, spoke of Egypt. She spoke of caravans. She spoke of India. She spoke of the Himalayas and a beautiful valley where we would stay for some time.

She spoke of the living Masters who were expecting me. She spoke of the Wesak and the Buddha. She spoke of the tide of energy rising to meet me from all these points in the world — rising from the Earth itself and rising from human hearts that I might bring down the pure light to meet them, joined with the blossoming of Mary as God's energy in the world.

We thanked them both and we were joyous, filled with excitement and expectant joy. That night we had a feast with all of our local friends and we told them, at least temporarily, goodbye. That night as we lay together we began to speak and I said, "My beloved, I feel the call to be joined with you in the Holy Temple of the Jews in Jerusalem, that all the world might see our union and be glad." Mary knew that it was perfect. Oh, that precious reflection of my heart! I placed a kiss on her beautiful nose where all the freckles lived, and my smile was gigantic.

I felt lit from within that she knew me so well and that we were in such perfect accord. In the soft night as a spring breeze came through the window, I turned to her and we Made Love again, exploding forth into the glorious experience of the whole of God and the great moment of ecstatic energy that is the Beginning. We knew ourselves truly as The Word, the two tones of the One Voice, singing forth into the cosmos a new song of Love.

That whole night we spent awake, flying through the realms of God, one heart singing those two songs together and creating a new song for the world. When morning came we spiraled in together creating truly a Double Helix, the foundation of life for a New World of Love, and we brought it into the world perfectly.

Such nights were to us the greatest blessing and they happened at every point where we were truly meant to bring that energy and anchor it to the Earth. But at that point we didn't know this and we were amazed by that which we had just experienced. As dawn colored the sky, we rose and went out together to walk. We went to the well and smiled at the women there, although the village was as yet quiet.

Delivering our buckets to my parents' porch, we went on walking outward, traveling out into the fields and the hills of Galilee that I loved so much, watching the sheep and the shepherds and seeing the grass sparkling with the diamonds of the early morning dew. Out from our heart poured such blessings that every animal raised its head and acknowledged us in the one voice in which all life communes, the voice of the living spirit.

We laughed together and greeted them — every sheep, every bird, every rabbit. Holding hands we walked into the olive groves and sat beneath their gnarled limbs. We were fed so completely by the nourishment of God that we were full, truly, to overflowing, filled with bliss and an ecstasy almost overwhelming to the both of us. In that sunlit morning in the gentle rolling hills of Galilee, it was hard to even imagine a whole world out there waiting for us, and a great work before us to do.

We took this moment for ourselves, turning to each other tenderly and when Mary, my Magdalene, brought her lips to mine, I knew God's Love tangibly and I danced with the Goddess intimately in the sunlight. When we rose, our hearts were so filled with gladness that we felt they had truly taken wing and gone out before us as messengers, bringing forth God's Message of beauty, unity and joy.

On our walk back we spoke again of the arc of time and we talked about the awareness of the pendulum — of how that which came through us would be subjugated to the judgments of men. An Age would pass before the feminine would rise again and our true story would be heard and the union of the One as two energies could occur.

Yet in that moment it hardly seemed possible that such distortions could occur. The presence of Our Creator was so alive within us and such a living part of our world. "Remember, Jeshua," Mary said to me, as her toe made designs in the Earth, "that many hearts are weary and many people are oppressed, and not many have felt Love like ours." Taking her hands I looked into her eyes, those eyes as green as gems, and I said, "My beloved, I know you are right. It is time to go forth and heal them. Let us lift up their hearts and show them that God, the living One, the one breath, can sing us all into perfection if we will let Her/Him."

She laughed at my inability to express through gender that which is so far beyond it. She said, "My beloved, my Jeshua, you don't need to use words with me." Our eyes met and our hearts joined and our ears heard not only the sheep bleating on the hillsides around us but heard that voice of the spirit within telling us to take forth this Love and let it be known.

And so we did. We returned to my parents house, to my family and said goodbye to my brothers and sister. I held my mother for the longest time. I was always awed by her. When I hugged my beloved Joseph, father of my heart and conduit for my awareness of the living masculine, I could only bow my head in honor to him and all that he continued to live. He understood me perfectly. We didn't need words. He clasped my shoulders and kissed my forehead and with this parting, Mary and I turned and left, and set our feet again on the pathway that the Creator placed before us.

We each carried a small pack made of soft and supple sheepskin and in it we had some traveling food and a couple of different robes. Everything else we trusted God to provide. We knew that life was abundant and we trusted our hearts to open the way for us through other hearts and through the abundance of the Earth. As we walked, the flowers nodded their heads, the animals sang their perfect notes of Love and our hearts understood every one of them as life's chorus sang the Creator's blessings. Our journey had begun perfectly and in joy.

May you know the unspeakable beauty
of the Love of the Beloved
in your heart and soul
and feel the warmth and richness
of that embrace.

Chapter Eleven

"The deepest truth of your heart is your Twin Flame's Love..."

There is a danger that arises when people think of Twin Flame Love. That danger is of the mind of the sub-creation on Earth, what we are calling the ego. It can take over the dream of Love and claim it as something for the personality rather than keeping the full awareness of the heart. Twin Flame Love is part of the living hologram of God and never can be separate in any way from the living Love that is the whole.

But the ego — that which dominates these lives that you live on Earth — has felt separate from God's Love for so long that the dream of the personality is to find at last the one who loves you to make you finally feel whole and loved. In other words, it places on the Twin Flame that which is God's alone. It is God's Love that makes you whole, that satisfies you, that brings you peace, grace and security. To look for this in the world is reversing the truth. It is part of the separation from God.

So please be aware when I speak of this Love, of its power and its beauty and its ecstasy — never, not ever for one moment was our Love separate from God. Never did we think it was for us alone or that we could take shelter in each other in any way. We were aware from that first moment when we touched as adults and felt the whole movement of Creation's Love with us, that everything in our Love was made for service, for the blessing and awakening of this precious world. Every moment we lived and breathed it together.

Each of us had always been fully alive to the Creator, fully aware of His/Her living presence as an integral part of our lives and aware of the context of our lives in this powerful moment of service that we had come to perform. The life of an awakened Twin Flame heart is fully infused with God's presence and dedicated with every breath to giving Love, peace and awakening to all.

When Mary and I Made Love, it was like Making Love with the entire cosmos, for there was nothing separate from us. We merged in the experience of the ongoing orgasm of Creation as it explodes in joy and wraps all life in ecstasy. We joined with all that is awake and present in that glorious ever-moving star-filled wholeness of Light.

Whether we came together on a hilltop or in a garden or in a cave or in a little hut somewhere, each touch, every breath that we shared was always open to the living whole. We are still and always perfect Love, God's Love being extended.

When your heart calls you to your Twin Flame, your first work is in the spirit, making sure that you are completely alive to God's presence always and releasing all dreams of a special Love that will sustain you, that will support you, help you, hold you up. These are the dreams of the ego that will rob you of your true vision and the Real experience of Twin Flame Love that is inseparable from the living whole, the sweet perfection of God's glory that is meant to live and breathe and give through you as a living heart.

I would ask you, each one of you, to bring your heart to God and let it be washed clean of any desires of the little self for Love in a limited way. In this way, you will truly be ready to be infused with this great and ever expanding experience of Real joy. I also say to you that bodies are an after-thought. They are such a small part of your true experience. They are, in fact, the illusory corner of the great being of Love that you are.

I ask you to reach for the truth of the Real magnificent Twin Flame union that many of you are even now beginning to experience beyond the illusion of life on Earth. Let that be the ground of your experience, that you might move beyond the veil of the ego dream and truly be available as a conduit for Love and for the Creator's world of wholeness.

Then, when you touch in the physical, the experience of Real union will be so grand for you, as it was for Mary and me, that the body will simply be infused with the truth of the spirit and be joined as part of the living orgasm that Creation is. The Creator's Love, God's Love, so intimate and yet so powerful, will fuse you in a unity of ecstatic joy beyond anything a mind can imagine.

With this also comes the deep awareness that you are part of the living whole and that nothing is ever really separate from you. Just as the heart is not separate from the body, neither is the heart of God separate from the living Whole. Every part functions in a unity of Love and giving that is so profound it is beyond describing. You, beloved friends, are part of this.

I wanted to take this moment, this aside, to say these things to you so that you would not look at this as just a simple Love story or be longing for someone to make you whole. The wholeness that you are already is so vast and so magnificent that I entreat you to reach for this. Then let that experience of truth in the spirit — the fact of the Twin Flame heart giving, pumping life into the glorious matrix of living Light — let that become so Real to you that it stands before you in the world.

For me, I did not know I was preparing for this, but my days and nights with God under the open skies, feeling the voice, tasting the vision, dissolving into that great movement of Love and sensing a unity, a union bigger than even I could encompass — all of these things were preparing me for Mary and for the moment of our coming together.

From the moment that we touched on that street when I returned from the first leg of my travels, from that moment when our eyes and our hearts met, everything we were together was yearning outward in service, pouring Love to every precious life trapped within the illusion of separation from our beloved Creator.

When we took our Love into the temples, into the community of the Essenes, into all the halls of wisdom and spiritual learning, everything we found simply upheld what we had experienced in our spirits together. In those days the truth of the Twin Flame was recognized everywhere. It was very much a part of the teachings of Egypt. It was alive in the ashrams of India, although that wasn't their name at the time. It lived and breathed totally in the Goddess culture where the Goddess and her consort were always Twins and relationships between men and women were honored and held in reverence.

It was only with the coming of "Christianity," the power usurped in my name by the ego, that the separation was created between spirit and body, and between man and woman. But you can see just how perfect for the ego this was, and how it was the next step on that spiral downward into the morass of darkness and separation for humanity. The ego, in order to continue the dream of separation from God, must separate you from everything good and beautiful and everything that is the truth of your soul.

The deepest truth of your heart is your Twin Flame's Love. It is part of your being. It is how God made you. So what a coup for the ego, the little mind to have created the illusion that men and women could never really come together and that Love was difficult and problematic and even sinful, and that the spirit and the body were separate, and the body is not filled with Light.

Our work, my dear friends, you whose hearts have called you to this great heralding trumpet of reunion, is to bring back together all that has been made separate, that the truth of God may finally be present in the world and everything can be seen as The One, The One God, everlasting and holy and absolutely beautiful.

In the world today, men and women have become opposites and the spirit and the body are not joined. The world and "the Heavens" seem to be two different things when in truth, it is all one life. The call goes forth now for Twin Flame hearts to reunite in the world. They are already together in the truth of God. As these seeming opposites come back to center and remember that Love is unity, then too will the body and the spirit once again merge and you will see dancing Lights within all of it. All of it is spirit.

When this occurs in your hearts, then the illusion of the ego will fall away because its existence is based upon the split — the split with God, the split between man and woman, the split between Heaven and Earth. The magnetic call is now so powerful that anyone whose heart is open must hear it, and you are hurtling toward your Twin Flame reunion at light speed.

Yet what must occur for this to happen is the transformation of all beliefs in separation so that the true union can be remembered all the way into the world. The world then will have the heart that it is meant to. You are the heart of the world, beating, and the world is totally made of Love and nothing else.

Thus, by the power of your Love and ours, mine with my beloved Mary, all opposites come back to the center. The pendulum can at last stop swinging from man to woman, Divine Masculine to Divine Feminine. It can come back to the center and to the Twin Flame, and all hearts can remember God and wholeness.

This is what we are about and it is coming. It is already here in the truth of Love. Your work is to release all that impedes you on this journey. The first place to start is with that longing for Love, that longing to have Love for yourself, to finally be loved for who you really are. The truth is the ego will never allow this and in the spirit you are already loved perfectly.

I am here to help you drop the search for Love. Now this may sound contradictory but the search is based on a false premise. It is based on the belief that you can be separate from something that is part of who you are.

The search for the Twin Flame has to fall away before the Real union can occur. I urge you to place your focus on our glorious beloved Creator, for that Love is the Love that makes you whole. The Twin Flame is part of your wholeness, already there, fully present and accounted for — just invisible to the ego-eyes of your personality.

As every belief in suffering and in the power of Love to wound you falls away, then the truth will be revealed, the truth that it is already there. You will feel it living within your spirit and pulsing through your being in utter joy. When you feel this and you are resting in the Love that is ever yours from God, then the Twin Flame will make itself known before you because there can be no separation of world and spirit when you are whole.

As Mary and I went forth in service, we knew that the Web, the Net of Light that we were holding, was the truth of Love set forth in vibration, singing as a force field of Light. By touching it, any heart would find itself freed from the illusion — be it the illusion of suffering, illness, of body or spirit or the illusion of separation from the mating of the spirit which is true Love, whole and Real.

In those days most marriages were marriages of convenience. But when the spirit is awakened, relationships change. They become infused with the

Light beyond the veil, and suddenly Love is right there within sight. So we watched as husbands and wives saw each other for the first time truly, and hearts remembered that they were part of a greater Light. The veil of the illusion of separate personalities was dissolved, at least for a moment, and a glimpse of the great sunlight of God's Love was revealed. In that moment bodies were healed, lives restored, riches returned and minds mended. All of it was simply from touching what we had woven from the Light and set forth to hold firmly between us.

Each day upon rising we would sing hymns to God's grace and thank God for the endless Love of our spirits. We would place our whole being in total dedication to the Light, and then we would hold hands and sit in stillness, allowing the Light to fully penetrate. Giving our hearts completely, we would re-dedicate all that we were and are and shall be forever. Truly we became a transparent heart beating together. Even our physical hearts became aligned, heartbeat-to-heartbeat, and we literally breathed the same breath in the same moments.

Yet we still appeared as man and woman in two bodies. But we knew with every fiber of our being that we were one heart. When people would see us when we emerged from our sitting, tears would spring into their eyes at our beauty and the beauty of our Love. Hardly anyone escaped this profound healing in our presence, healing of the belief in Love.

The powerful force of God's presence was always with us and always included in everything we said and did. We often spoke to others of not making the mistake of thinking that Love was something for them personally, but rather recognizing that Love was part of their spiritual truth and their experience with God in eternity. When this truth could be felt and trusted, then it would be experienced also in the world.

The time has come for the great healing, for the circle to be complete and for all that has been dreamed as being separate to be released and re-experienced as unity. Because we walked the dusty roads of Earth, fed our bodies and slept beneath the stars, and loved as physical lovers and as SoulMates, we know truly that of which we speak when we say that Love will open up the world to unity. The illusion of Heaven and Earth will fall away and Heaven, truth, Love, glory, unity, peace will be the Reality because God is ever and only one thing. Not Earth and spirit but one Love everywhere just waiting for the sweet remembrance.

We are here to help you find this yourself.

Surrender into the Beloved
and discover the quintessence of Love.
Be suspended in the
sweetness from
which we were formed.

Chapter Twelve

"I hold the torch for womankind all over the world..."

Mary Magdalene speaks:

I come today to speak as the Divine Feminine and to hold the torch for womankind all over the world. I hold up this light of power, purpose and freedom, and say to all of you that I know "you can do it." I know you can find your inner spark, your strength, your womanhood and the emanation of God that you embody — that which we name the Goddess or the great Feminine.

I know this Light, Her Love, as a living part of me, and that which brings forth the sweet Earth and weaves Her breath with the wind, Her laughter in the change of the seasons. She speaks with many voices — the animals, the elements, all of Nature. She also speaks within us and moves as a living flame through our countenance and draws the truth from our mouth.

I call to you, my beloved sister friends, and tell you that you have a very great and important part in holding the center, in bringing the balance for humankind and holding the Light of purpose for the Divine Masculine as we enter into this time of rebirth.

It is just as if humanity were in the living womb of God and you are making ready to be born into a new reality, that which you are naming the New World. But it is really much greater than this, for as you know, it is the return of humanity to its innocence. By this I mean its pristine state of Love. Not innocence the way the world looks at innocence — as somebody who can be taken advantage of. Rather, I speak of an innocence that is fresh and new like a brand new morning that sparkles with the morning dew, in which the voice of Love speaks clearly and brings forth the Love and power of God, Goddess, the One.

Now I will pick up the thread of our tale, joining the narrative of my beloved Jeshua, the man who stole my heart from the moment I saw him as a young boy, laughing on the hills of Galilee, just as he stole the hearts of men. He was a man who carried such unearthly joy and beauty and such Light within his eyes that every life who came near, who encountered him, truly was transformed.

The topic is our wedding in the Great Temple of the Jews in Jerusalem. We had sent invitations by word of mouth and some written in careful calligraphy to those potentates and people of worldly importance whom we knew must be witness to the expression of that which together we were bringing to the world.

Our families were excited. Our friend, Elizabeth, the mother to John who later became known as the Baptist, came out of the hills and her silence to come and plan with us and to make it a joyous and beautiful wedding. Though we had already celebrated our Love in many ways and then united in the community of the Essenes, we knew that it was important to be wed in Jerusalem.

It was a statement that we were making that would carry the energy of our Twin Flame heart, our union as a form of worship, through all the Ages of human darkness and the pushing aside of the feminine — even the burying of our story as lovers, partners and Twin Flames, until the time was right.

As spring came to the hills of Galilee, we collected our worldly goods and set out to walk through Samaria and down into Judea and to Jerusalem. We gave ourselves a month to do this because we knew we had much to see along the way. Not so much the land, although we loved it and it spoke to us, but those people who had a part to play in the drama that was meant to unfold around us.

As we walked, my beloved looked out on the world with eyes that saw it all — not just the physical world, but every stratum of Light and consciousness. As I watched him, I could see the Love in his eyes as he poured his heart out to humanity. His eyes carried a Light that bared the souls of men and made women bow at his feet. Yet, his heart was so pure that there was no ego — just the pure Love of God shining as a blessing on every life.

I would watch him as we would crest a hill, standing in the green grass surrounded often by the sweet sheep and the lonely shepherds. He would gaze out across the hills and valleys and I knew that he was seeing far beyond the normal vision, seeing the movements of Light in the world and bowing in service to the awakening of Love.

At that time of the world there was so much darkness. There was little to recommend humankind except for those pockets of great Light and awareness that were the anchors of the Masters. Such centers existed everywhere, but shown especially brightly in Egypt and India. Humankind itself was a raging war of greed and avarice and despair. Every moment I would see him with that look in his eyes, I would take his hand and join him with my heart. The moment I did, the Creator's Love would sweep through us and wash the world with such Love and grace that it would bring me literally to my knees in gratitude.

I would kneel upon the Earth and pray: "Beloved Goddess, lift them to Your bosom and let every soul remember Your loving kindness and the Light that lives within them." My beloved would place his hand upon the crown of my head and I could feel the Love pouring to me. It contained all the Love I am and have poured to Jeshua for I love him with my whole being and I truly worship at his feet.

I would gently lay my hand upon his sandals and rub my fingers along his toes. Through him I would feel the great Light and power of God meeting the sweet Earth. I would feel that meeting right down to my toes and I knew I was witness to a miracle — the true Light of God incarnate as a savior to humanity and a Light for the world.

I want to tell you about the light in his eyes as he looked outward in those times — the power and beauty that I saw emanate from him. His eyes were as blue as a cerulean sky. The light shone out from them, great rays lifting the fog from humanity and seeing through every person to the depths of their heart and soul. These were moments of spontaneous grace and prayer and they happened to us very often. We were humbled at the power moving through us, the power of the Love of the living Goddess.

I would feel it in my whole being and in my body as if I were cracked open and became only a vehicle of Her Love. Sometimes when this Light was upon us and when the power of this Love pulsed through our hearts, we would find the privacy of an olive grove or a stand of trees and we would lay our cloaks out upon the grass and come together in holy matrimony. To me this is the meaning of real marriage. It is not something that you do once and then forget. It is the giving of your being, your heart, your energy, every bit of who you are continuously, and renewing that vow regularly in the meeting of heart, mind and spirit until you become together that great eternal Love-Making of the Creator.

To say the Earth moved can't even contain our experience. To say the Heavens opened before us isn't enough. But you can sense what happens in a Twin Flame union when it is brought all the way to the Earth and the power and the purpose of the living Love become who we are and what moves us. Such an experience of Making Love is as elemental as the wind. It is the sweeping power of the Creator moving through us and bringing us together. It had little to do with Jeshua and Mary the Magdalene and the personalities that we carried.

En route to Jerusalem, we came, after some time, to the town of Joppa and to the home of Joseph whom you know as Joseph of Arimathea. We were welcomed, and I beheld the Love of Joseph and Jeshua. I knew I was witnessing true friends. It was as if I could see the world move through their Love for it and the excitement that they had in sharing. They sparked each other and began speaking of weighty things and of the great movement of God that was happening.

Joseph knew the truth about me and Jeshua, and welcomed me with loving arms. He brought us into his beautiful house that was wrapped with stone the color of sand, walls that contained lovely gates that opened into magical gardens that even had little ponds. They took my fancy right away. They were filled with benches and places to sit in peace. I knew that I would spend much time in this beautiful oasis of Nature.

Joseph and Jeshua, with broad smiles and arms around each other's shoulders, rushed into the house and began to speak of deep philosophies. I could tell they had forgotten me in their hurry to share their friendship and their Love and their intelligence. I gave thanks to The One for this friend that God had given to my Jeshua, for I knew that such friends were going to be of value beyond anything that the world could give to us, even gold. This was a man who obviously had such vision and understood that Star that rose above Bethlehem. He knew the workings of the turning of the Ages and the message that Jeshua brought. He also acknowledged the beauty of the Divine Feminine and knew that our Love and marriage had an important place.

That night as we sat in this airy house on furniture he had imported from Persia, feet resting on cool tile floors and our hands holding drinks in the most beautiful pottery, he spoke to us of all that he had received directly from the movement of the living Spirit. He said to us both that he honored and supported our Love.

Turning to Jeshua, looking him deeply in the eyes, he said: "I will always be here to support your beloved Mary, the Magdalene. Know that I am hers from this moment on, just as I am yours. Know too, my beloved friend," as he took Jeshua's hand in his, leaning toward him so he could reach, "I will be with both of you every step of the way as this divine dance is executed, and I will be for you the greatest support that I possibly can in those moments that shall make history. I know who you are."

Jeshua placed his hands then upon Joseph's head and said, "My friend, God bless you. I bring to you all the glory of My Father/Mother now and in every moment, and call to the Angels to support you in your service to life. I am so grateful that you are part of the dance and also that you are my dearest and deepest friend." I could feel the presence of the Beings of Light and the Angels whispering in my ear that this was a man who had powerful vision and the strength to hold the truth of us, and I was so glad.

That night we lay in cool sheets on a bed made of rattan — sheets that I believe were woven in Egypt and pillows that were filled with down or something that was the softest thing upon which I had ever laid my head. The night breathed through the open window. All the lovely night-time insects buzzed around our heads and sang to us of Her Love and the song of Love held by the Angels that was offered in that moment to us.

I realized as I touched my beloved, his velvet skin, as soft as that night's darkness, that there were many ways of Making Love. This movement of our hearts was one as we rose on pillars of living Light, entwining our spirits and singing of Love until we came to the place where the glorious Creator lives, that purest, highest, most sublime vibration. We allowed God to bless us in our union of spirit, life force and the elemental energies of our being. Then, together we brought it down in a great Helix of Light into the world.

All of these things were simply spontaneous, although Jeshua had studied many things. He would often smile and turn to me and say, "My beloved Mary, I knew none of this before you. I am an open book before your Love. Teach me." I would smile and my heart would open and the Love of the living Goddess would pour through me to bless him. We would know in our hearts and our beings what we were meant to be and to do each moment, perfectly.

That night we loved each other as spiritual beings and left the physical to itself, knowing we are embodiments of Light and energy anyway. This was always our experience, whether we held hands or Made Love or danced in fields of Light. It was truly all one thing.

The next morning we rose with the sunrise, filled with delight. The moment Jeshua and Joseph saw each other, they began again speaking of the Talmud and all of the wisdom of the Jews and speaking of the great Masters, teachers, who came up through Egypt and the great wise beings of Light who sat in the caves in India. They spoke of the patterns of destiny and that which we were meant to out-picture.

But they also laughed and joked with each other, tickling each other with their knowledge of each man's personality and the truth of his being. I simply watched, filled with such happiness, to see my beloved with his close friend and to know that we had such a wise person for support in the expression of Love we were here to bring.

We had both seen clearly what was coming for Jeshua and for me as I held his energy, that he might raise up the world. But knowing didn't change our joy because the world and the spirit were so in unison, one great movement of Love, with very indistinct separation. The world truly was dancing Light for us and of course, the realms of God were living Love. They interwove into each other and created the Earth in which we lived. There was no sense of dread or heaviness in us but rather destiny inspired us and brought us all to the Creator's faith in us to carry out this important mission.

As we spent time with Joseph we visited his many estates. We also went together to the seashore. This was one of the greatest delights for me. In the ocean, oh, how I felt the Mother's Love! I could hear Her voice speaking. I could feel the life blood of the Earth as it moved in waves and connected with all human beings, touching the shores of distant lands and becoming a field of the dreams and hopes of men and women.

We also had the greatest fun as we ran up and down the shore of the Mediterranean and watched as the ocean reflected the sky and the sky became the ocean. Jeshua turned to me, reached out his hand and said, "Mary, let's run!" We took off down the sand, laughing, holding each other, bumping together until we fell and rolled over and over, our limbs intertwined, ending in a beautiful kiss. As we lay there embracing,

Joseph arrived, walking up to us and said to us, "You two are so beautiful, and though I have a wife I will not know such a Love. But I am blessed by it in you."

He was so wise and truly carried the consciousness of the Highest, anchored in his form. He saw a map of the world and of the coming of the Light so clearly and powerfully that his eyes, though dark like the richest chocolate, held a similar vision to Jeshua's. I could feel their energies vibrating in a synchronicity of purpose that moved me. Such glorious days we spent with Joseph, just playing in the playground of the world, dipping our feet, swimming in the Mediterranean, running down the beach in wet robes and dancing in the sunset. As the lights streamed in the wet sand and made us catch our breath, it was so beautiful.

Then we rode home in a sweet little carriage that belonged to Joseph, very unusual for that day, similar to the chariots of the Romans, complete with Roman horses. We delighted in all the things the world could provide and had provided to Joseph. But the center of it all was the one you know as Jesus — so strong and straight and true and beautiful. Well, yes, I am slightly biased.

His hair was streaming in the wind, streaked even more blond by the sun so that many shades of gold were evident and his eyes saw such distances and such visions of God that made me shiver to look in them. I watched also as Joseph brought his friends, friends from all over the world, for Joseph was a well-traveled man. As they came it was obvious that he had spoken of Jeshua. All of them bent their knee and told us that they gave us their fealty and their support of our mission. We began to see what a web of Light God had woven through the instrument of Joseph of Arimathea. We realized that Joseph was a living mystery school in and of himself.

These figures who are history to you were the people who filled our lives and made us aware that we were rich beyond anything we would have imagined as God brought us new friends and allies.

As the time of the wedding approached, we knew we must leave soon for Jerusalem. Joseph gathered as many friends as he could under his roof — the same house in which we had been staying — and he asked Jeshua to speak. Jeshua said, "The bells of Heaven are ringing. It is a new era for humankind and I have come to be the bridge between the world and the Creator. As the Heavens dance in their symphony of Love, the stars move into a new course. This course will be the evolution through much time and many changes in the world. That which we do here in the coming years will be the foundation for everything, for every change and every opening to the Creator's Love, built upon the patterns of what came before, acknowledging them all, but becoming even more as a gift to humanity.

"I come to bring a structure of Light, a wheel of living Love that can support a new evolution. Upon this pattern of Light, this living matrix of God, shall be built the world's transcendence and the purity of the Light that lives within it. I am that which stitches together the perception of duality and brings the mending of the world's quilt that is all the beautiful and diverse peoples and all of their heart's beliefs — all the ways that they have touched God. I come to sew them all together and to create a blanket of Love for humankind in which they can be warm and safe and find their true Home.

"That is why I ask for your blessing, dear friends, you who are the friends of Joseph of Arimathea. I ask for your support for myself and for my beloved, my Mary, the Magdalene, because these times we have been shown will be dangerous and many will lose their lives. But those who hold closely to God's plan will be safe and strong and carry the Light that will light the world for Love.

"To all of you we give our gratitude and we thank you for your support. Most of all, we ask you to find your own way to worship the One who moves the Heavens and infuses the world, that that great wisdom and Love can provide your course, open you to the hands of destiny and let your heart speak the truth of you out into the world."

He took each person's hand in his and looked deeply into each one's eyes and said, "The great living One, the All of the Universe, gives you the blessing of a true and pure life of service. For this we thank you and I bless you in the Father-Mother's name. And so it is. Amen."

I rose and spoke also and I said, "The Goddess is here, She who is the movement of the Divine Feminine. While it seems that the power of the world is shifting to the men, don't be fooled. The Goddess is ever present and She shall rise again. The Temples to the Goddess are now still strong, but they will soon be waning. So I ask each of you to take this token of Her

Love." I gave forth tiny jewels for each man to hold in his hand.

I saved one for the wife of Joseph. I said, "Great and loving Goddess, join these hearts of men with the movement of Your great Feminine Love that they might be balanced in every step and especially in their hearts as they come as servants for humanity and for the raising of the world into the expression of Your Love and Your grace. And so it is. Amen."

The next morning after our wonderful meeting in which we spoke deeply of the mission and of the energy that together we all were bringing, when we rose, Joseph had packed many things. He had given us new robes and new sandals which were very important in those days. The leather was strong and thick and the workmanship beautiful. Mine even had gold inlays and I thought, what a blessing God has wrought in this man.

We donned our new clothes and joined Joseph to break our fast, eating cakes of grain and goat cheese, drenched in honey, followed by figs and dates. Then we knelt together in prayer in the middle of the room. You could hear then the silence and our breathing as we opened into the Light and the Love.

After we felt the movement of Love between us, aligning us perfectly, Jeshua and I rose and faced Joseph. Taking his hands in ours, looking into his eyes, we said to him, "We are so blessed to know you and we will carry your Love with us every step of the way. First, of course, we will see you in Jerusalem in ten days. After that you will find that we will come to you at the twilight of each day and you will hear us in your spirit. We will speak to you through our hearts. You will know that we are joined always in the Creator's Love."

With this we kissed Joseph's cheeks, first me, then Jeshua, and wrapped our arms around him together. I had tears in my eyes as we prepared to embark, tears for the honor of knowing such a man and knowing that Jeshua had such a friend. "Thank You, God, Thank You, Goddess. Thank You, Father, Mother of All for this blessing of our Joseph, for his gift in our lives. Bless him and support him in the greatest ways that You possibly can. We Love You. Amen."

With some reluctance we all walked out of the door, down the path and out the gate and stood in that dusty street, saying our last goodbyes for the day. We turned ourselves to the East and South and headed for Jerusalem and our wedding.

The purity surrounds and receives
my surrendered soul,
as if it were the only offering
of this precious moment circling
into an intimacy
that enfolds me in forever.

Chapter Thirteen

"Son of Light, Son of the Morning, he who brings the world back to Love..."

Jeshua speaks:

As we set out to arrange our wedding in the Temple in Jerusalem and the season turned toward the summer solstice, things began to happen on the inner planes of our being. For me, something came alive in my heart — a new light, a new flame burning, that lit for me a deeper commitment in my service to humanity and granted me a wordless understanding that a new power was being born on Earth, as it is in the realms of God. The moment of this birth was to be our wedding in Jerusalem.

While our wedding in the community of the Essenes was holy and beautiful, there was something about this wedding in the Holy Temple in Jerusalem that moved me to my soul. It truly shook my foundations and opened up my life in new ways, allowing me to see greater patterns of life and Light and power and beauty and Love, and our part in it. The lineage of the Jews and their part in the world history, and the sacredness of the Temple and the Light burning there, gave me a deep awareness of the new pattern that Mary and I were on Earth to bring.

It was a beautiful summer morning as we walked. The air was infused with Light and the wings of bees and the sweet messages of the insects and flowers. We were filled with delight. Waving to every traveler, I spoke surreptitiously to all the donkeys and every goat and sheep and pig and sang beneath my breath the serenade of Nature, and my singing was acknowledged in fullness. My beloved Mary looked at me and laughed, and said, "Oh, Jeshua, there you go again, singing that song of life."

I also laughed and grabbed her, picked her up and swung her round and round in circles in the middle of that dusty road, my sandals filling with soft dust and kicking up a cloud of it. The hem of my robe became dust colored. The laughter that rose within me was met by the Celestial Ones, until the voice of the cosmos was singing our song. I felt deeply the blending of the world as it appeared to the mind, with the great movement of the cosmos of God's Love.

As we arrived in Jerusalem, I felt the call coming from the Temple and knew that I must honor it. We planned to make a visit to my dear friends, Lazarus and Mary and their family in Bethany, before the wedding. Mary wanted to gather together some things from the market to take as gifts. She knew, as I did, that my time at the Temple was something that I alone needed, deep inside. I needed to acknowledge my Jewish heritage before I joined it to the greater world as a conscious weaving of a new unity for humankind. So Mary left me at the Temple and we agreed to meet later at the marketplace.

When I arrived at the Temple, I was greeted by the old Rabbi who had eyes that to the world might seem blind, but, oh, his vision of the inner life was extra clear and he saw everything! When he saw me, he said, "Son of Light, Son of the Morning, he who brings the world back to Love. I am here forever in your service. I bow to you and honor your chosen beloved, Mary, the Magdalene."

I grasped his shoulders and placed a kiss on his forehead, and said to him, "My beloved elder, my beloved Mary and I would like to be joined here in the Temple." I was honest with him and told him that we had been joined by the Essenes. He was a man of true holiness and said that we had his deepest blessing, and that God had shown him that we were coming to Jerusalem for this purpose. This majestic and very holy man who spent his days and nights in worship honored our Love. We set the date for the banns of matrimony.

He stared at me unseeing for many minutes, and in those minutes I felt his heart reach out. The moment our hearts connected I knew he saw everything — through my eyes but also through the great eye of God. I saw the rising of the great *Caduceus*, the healing of the world through the Divine Masculine and Divine Feminine coming together at the apex as the pinnacle, the healing of the one life from all duality. He, my beloved Zacharia, not only Elder of the Temple but also Elder of many things including the Halls of Light, took my arm and I let him guide me.

He said, "I am to take you into the inner Temple, into the Sanctuary of the High Holy One that you might dedicate yourself to the One at the Tabernacle of the merging of all aspects of humanity and all the array of races, types and bodies. You are that Tabernacle of God in the flesh and you must honor the Holy One. Even though the rules of men would prohibit this, the rules of God that speak in my heart say otherwise."

Before I could protest, he took my hand, parted the curtain and led me in. I stood before the altar facing the Torah that was so filled with radiant Light I could not behold it. I realized it was no longer physical but had become the pure expression of that place where the living One, the All of Love, the Creator and humanity meet.

I cannot even speak of the things that happened there, that brought me into a deeper communion but also a deeper, much deeper commitment to that Living One and to being the one living Tabernacle, where God and humanity meet in the heart. I also understood with all my being what marriage truly meant and what it meant to me. I saw and felt and was that moment of explosive Light when the movement of the Creator brought forth this Love into the great panorama of life and relationship that we live. To it all, I said, "Yes. Let us be this and let me honor the sanctity of this union. God, I understand this is the beginning of our greater work, of our destiny, and I am ready. I give you my life, my heart, my soul, my being. Take me."

I was lost in the Light in such exquisite and glorious ecstasy that I have no idea how much time went by as the world reckons it. When I opened my eyes at last, the Rabbi was still there, lost in his own ecstatic reverie of the Light. I also saw the circles of Angelic presences, hundreds, thousands deep all around me. They spoke to me with one voice and said to me, "Jeshua. You are to be the power of Light in the world. For this we honor you with every breath of The One and sing your name as part of The One's Holy Song. We weave together your heart with your beloved Mary, the Magdalene, that all the world might see the truth of the God of Love as He/She is made manifest in the world."

I was overcome with reverence for the beauty of God as it expresses in all the realms of Light and life and movement, especially as it expresses in this world and in this union of the masculine and the feminine. I saw in that moment clearly what we were mending. Though I had understood the decision that humanity had made that created the separation from God, in that moment I saw the incessant downward spiraling of that energy of the reversal of life on Earth as it built and moved. I also saw the ways that we could reverse the trend — walk back outward that inward turning spiral. I saw that it could only be done in the Twin Flame energies, the balanced manifestation of divine Love.

My heart exploded with prayers of gratitude and I said, "God, You are the endless One and I am forever Yours and I give myself to my beloved as well in worship of You, together, as this heart that is sanctified by You and Your very act of Creation." When I emerged I knew that I stretched from the Real of Love deeply into the Earth herself, and I was washed clean — so clean that I was the movement of Light, moving without volition toward the pulsing heart of Love that is the feminine, my beloved Mary. I took my leave of the Rabbi and the Temple and went to find the market, looking for my Mary and knowing if I didn't find her quickly, all I had to do was open my heart and my heart would lead me right to her.

It is the truth that we are all connected by this Web of Light. It is alive with the hum of consciousness and living joy, and everything is ever and always available to all of us in every moment. Knowing as we did that we were not ever really separate, our hearts were like homing beacons, finding each other instantly and effortlessly, no matter where our bodies happened to be. If we needed to be together with each other physically, it was easy.

And this did occur. We picked up her gifts — some beautiful statuary, exceptional incense and packages of fruit and dates and special sweetmeats to take as treats. It was the custom to come bearing gifts any time our feet were to pass someone's mantel as friends. We wrapped these gifts in a beautiful cloth that Mary had purchased with the intention of making scarves for the women. She placed all of this in my pack and we began the journey to Bethany, a neighboring town to Jerusalem.

I kneel in reverence
overcome with gratitude
when I ponder the brilliance
of the divine design
of life in all
its infinite glory.

Chapter Fourteen

"I understood that he is the Oak King for humankind..."

Mary Magdalene speaks:

Jeshua had a burning desire in his heart to spend time with his dear friends, Lazarus and his family, in Bethany, and because he is my beloved and I desired never to be parted from him, I went with him and truly delighted in our stay. But I was already hearing the call of my own burning desire to go to the Temple of my sisters, those who worshiped with me and celebrated the Divine Feminine.

I spoke of this to Jeshua. While at first we felt we would rather stay together, it soon became clear that Jeshua, too, needed a time of meditation and time with his spirit family before the wedding. We ultimately agreed that I would travel to Jerusalem alone to be with my beloved sisters at the Goddess Temple to prepare myself for our wedding. I was excited to be on my way. We decided that Jeshua would walk with me part of the way back to Jerusalem.

Our journey passed so quickly and with such delight and joy that I was surprised, completely surprised, when we arrived at the crossroads where the road from the North met the East/West thoroughfare. We had named this the Star Crossing because the intersection of all four roads coming together at angles looked just like the rays of a star beam. In the center of the crossroads, someone had placed a sundial. We thought it a perfect symbol of the Light. We felt a special affinity for this place where all the roads met and every direction was possible from this place. It seemed appropriate to be the spot where we took leave from each other for just a little while.

As we stood in the afternoon sunlight, I gazed up at him and I saw the Light shining within him. His countenance was more radiant than any star, more radiant than the glorious sun that shone down upon us. In that moment, the spirit opened to us and I saw him as the deliverance of the world. I truly felt like the moon with the sun, reflecting its glorious Light. While my heart knew that we are one in the truth of God, to see him in such radiance was more than I could accept with my mind as part of my own being. Thus, I accepted the limitation of my Earthly view and simply gave him his due. Placing my hands on his heart, I said, "Jeshua, how blessed is the world to have you and how very blessed am I."

Thus we parted ways. We promised to see each other at least briefly before our wedding. He left and placed sweet kisses upon my eyes and said, "May God be with you, my beloved, my Mary. You know you have my heart and my soul." I joined with some other travelers and shared with them the beauty of Nature and the harmony of the living spirit. In this way I came to my time in the Goddess Temple, and my beloved Jeshua returned for his time in Bethany, to drink in the Love of these special people so close to him and find also his time of solitude and deepest meditation.

This day as I began my private journey toward our wedding, I felt simply overflowing with joy. We were soon to announce our union to the world and it was exciting. I knew that all my dearest friends and my family and Jeshua's were very much in support of this wedding. I looked forward to Jeshua's mother's face when she saw me in my bridal array. I felt my heart and my feet take wing.

On this summer day as the dust flew around me, and butterflies grazed my head, I skipped down that road to Jerusalem with joy bubbling up from within. As I passed the wonderful and simple folk upon the road, I greeted everyone effusively and announced to one and all, "I am going to Jerusalem for my wedding." I extended the invitation universally. I figured that everyone could come and if they didn't, they would witness in their hearts and spirit what was happening on the inner planes and it would nourish them.

I was welcomed by my sisters at the Temple with open arms and such Love, for I had spent all the years since my puberty with them and we were close, even closer than blood sisters. I had risen in the Temple easily, going through the initiations and becoming the embodiment of the Goddess. When I was present at the Temple, I often led the rituals and spoke to the acolytes and the lifetime servants of the Goddess, those women who had given their lives in service. I was known for wearing the mantle of the Magdalene which in many ways is the feminine version of Christ. It is she who has become the Light and Love of the Divine Feminine, the embodiment of the Goddess on Earth.

I entered the Temple to pray and to fast and to make myself cleansed on every level and ready to take my Jeshua in a marriage so deep and so cosmic that it encircled the whole world and marked the beginning of a new Age. When I entered the Goddess Temple to pray, I saw the candles flickering on the many faces of the Goddess, flowers bedecking her, overflowing to floor and altar. Everywhere I looked there was abundance of offerings — fruit on platters piled high, succulent and jewel-toned, every variety imaginable, offered to Her in Love.

The Sanctuary was truly splendid, and filled with such Light and color. It truly was a magical place. When one entered it, one immediately felt Her presence as an intimate caress of tender Love, soft and feminine by nature and yet strong and invincible. I knelt to pray and gave Her my heart, my life, my will in service and asked to truly be the Divine Feminine on Earth, taking in marriage my consort, my heart, my life, the Divine Masculine, the Twin Flame heart of God in this holy union to come.

As I prayed for her blessing I felt it, and I felt Jeshua's presence with me. I realized that this had become like my own breath. I felt him alive within me, so much a part of my very being that I could hear his thoughts and feel his presence, fulfilling the whole of me as nothing else could. I prayed prayers of gratitude for hours that day, feeling it so deeply that tears ran down my cheeks. I held the flower petals in my hand and felt their softness and the serenity that they brought. I felt a peace that I had never known.

As I left the Sanctuary I continued to pray as I walked out into the garden. The Temple had many gardens all of which were dedicated to different aspects of the Goddess as the world. Every one was beautiful in a totally different way and brought with it a very different feeling and a wholly different vibration. I went from garden to garden which was a holy journey that all of the women in the Temple walked every day. It was not only a daily communion with the faces of the One in Her feminine nature, but also a very intimate communion with Her, and it was wonderful.

Every step I heard Jeshua's name. I began to feel a rhythm of our union deeper than anything I had as yet known, more primitive in a way, as if it were rising from the very beginnings of the world, and claiming us as part of Her in all Her expressions in the world. I began to understand just how fully She is incarnated in every one of us, in every creature, in every energy, in every manifestation of Her Love as Nature — all of it speaking to each of us in just the perfect ways, moment-to-moment.

As I walked from garden to garden, I began to feel another pattern. It emerged beneath the color and the joy of the summer day and the Temple in its splendor. I stopped. I felt the Earth move and She began to speak and the voices of the elements joined Her. I found myself face down upon the Earth in the middle garden, half way through my garden walk. I felt as if all I could do was hold on as the Earth moved and everything that I had known came apart.

The patterns of life began to rearrange themselves. As life moved and split and swayed in this strange dance, I saw a chasm, a split between the Goddess and humanity. I understood that She must be incarnated in us, and that especially in the times to come, this would be forgotten. Then I saw in my inner vision the celebration of Candelmas and how that celebration honored the sacrifice of the elements, Nature and Earth and life in these patterns of separation. That which lives must die to be reborn to the Spirit.

I saw the Oak King as he wears the crown of thorns and gives himself as the year ends, that a new year and a new life and a new Light may be born into the world. Then I saw my Jeshua and I understood in an even deeper way just who he is — that he is the Oak King for humankind, the willing sacrifice that takes away the darkness that new Light may be born.

Though I had seen these things in my inner vision before and we both knew the role that he was born to, I began to understand the part I was to play in holding the true life in perfect Love, while the symbols of death and resurrection were before my eyes. In that moment I felt my heart breaking, even at the same time that it was ecstatic. I was here to serve the Will of the Goddess, no matter what, and I had the honor of serving with my Jeshua.

And yet, the visceral awareness of his death was upon me in a way I had never experienced before, as if I were being torn from limb to limb, my heart torn out. I lay upon that garden soil and wailed. As I did, I felt Her, the Goddess whom I love and serve, all around me and within me, and I felt Her Love infuse me in a way that I had never before felt. I have never felt as close to Her as I was in that moment. I comprehended what it was that Jeshua was doing in taking on the separation of humanity from the Living One — God, the intimate.

All the wheels of life and death had come forth from this separation. The only way to end this passion play of life and death and life again and death again was to end the mistake from which it had come. Someone had to be like the Oak King, the willing sacrifice for the bridging of this chasm I had been shown between the Creator and humanity.

Then I saw my beloved, stretched like a rainbow across the distance between God and human hearts. I watched as he took upon himself that distance and every stream of anguish that had come forth from it. With all his strength and might and dedication, with everything he was, he wrenched the chasm closed, sewing it together with his own body and his own spirit.

I saw that while he was the needle, I was the thread. It was up to me to make the sacrifice with him, and to bring it into embodiment in a way that was truly gentle and available to humanity and to the very real life that we lived daily. The luminosity of my Jeshua was beyond describing and the arc of his spirit beyond even my comprehension. Yet the world as the symbols of the Goddess, and the reckoning of the decisions of humanity and their new affirmation somehow must be woven into a tapestry of life and worship and connection with the heart.

This I understood was the place for the Divine Feminine, making all of this real and simple and understandable as a continual renewal of life, a rebirth of what is valuable. The upliftment into Love and grace must occur. Somehow through all of this I finally understood my place fully, that Jeshua was the bridge, but I, the materials with which he builds it. Suddenly our partnership made sense in a way that touched my deepest soul and my spirit and enlivened my heart within me.

In that moment I said, "Beloved Goddess whom I love and serve, I understand at last what You are asking of me and I give my life to You and to my beloved Jeshua and to the resurrection of the world into infinity and grace. I give this willingly and continually. I will affirm this every day. I go to my wedding understanding not only what I am bringing but what it is that we are here to do. I ask for Your blessing."

I felt a great wash of Light and tender Love. I felt God as Mother and as Father. I felt the Nameless One, the great Creator who is all things and how all were woven together as one life. I felt myself lifted to my feet and my chin lifted, my eyes brought up. When I opened them, above the walls of the garden I could see the sunset in every imaginable color — more colors than the rainbow, more colors than I had ever seen in any sunset, anywhere I had traveled.

I knew I was being given the sign and a blessing. I accepted it in reverence and gratitude. From that moment there lived within me a great peace that hadn't been there, and all the pieces of the pattern of our Twin Flame Light and service were before me in every moment effortlessly and within my heart. I never wavered from that moment on.

I know I haven't explained to you succinctly or even clearly those things that I experienced that day but trust me when I tell you, it was truly revolutionary and brought me the awareness of my journey with Jeshua in a whole new way. Until that time I had been shown these glimpses of the patterns and scenes from my life with Jeshua, and I had the intuition and the understanding of his death and the power of his resurrection. But it all was disjointed and it bothered me. I wavered sometimes in my dedication because I didn't understand the whole thing and exactly what it was we were doing for humanity.

From that moment in the garden of the Temple of the Goddess I understood completely what was happening, what we had promised, the pattern we were meant to bring and anchor in the world and the truth of Love that lived within us as a gift from the Creator to humankind.

My sisters in the Temple were anxious to celebrate and wanted to honor me with all of the rituals for the bride. I felt so humbled and alive in Her presence that I knew I couldn't visit with them at that moment. I must seek within and keep that communion going and honor the Goddess incarnated in me.

I spent many hours in the baths, anointing my body and watching the Light within it. I allowed Her to teach me directly in the spirit even more about the ways of divine Love-Making than even I had known. I had learned so much already about taking on the role of the Divine Mother and honoring the life of Her people in rituals of fertility and rituals of blessing. Now I learned my role in awakening Jeshua to the true power of his life as Divine Masculine and his Love for me.

In the baths and as I prayed and fasted and spent time in meditation, I was shown the deeper makings of Real magic, the power of Real and Sacred Love in recreating the world. I grasped that on the night of our wedding this is what we were being asked to do through our Love-Making — create a new pattern for humanity and a new foundation for the world. This is what I promised Her we would do.

We came to the day before the wedding, and I awoke breathless with anticipation just at the edge of dawn. The day broke. It was so beautiful, warm but not yet hot, although I knew that the heat was coming. I threw on my simple robe and belted it and with bare feet I ran out into the garden singing and laughing and shouting, "It is tomorrow and I am the handmaiden of the Goddess today!"

I knew that Mother Mary was coming, Jeshua's beloved and beautiful mother, and my mother as well. My mother and I were somewhat estranged, and I had far more affinity for Mary who was an Angel. She also was my mentor and my teacher and held for me like a tuning fork, the sound, the tone of the Goddess in the world. I don't know how to explain what she was and still is, except to tell you that she is the being who holds the energies of the Creator's purity and beauty.

While I was always earthy and lusty and passionate and a trickster in my own simple way, always exploring and into mischief and running, dancing, playing — Mary it seemed was born as pure divinity and never wavered. Every word that she spoke was the Goddess speaking and every moment in her presence was pure Love. I learned so much from simply sitting at her feet and listening.

Her Love for me was so unequivocal that in it I felt whole and blessed and accepted and seen in a way that no one else had seen me. Nor has anyone seen me thus except my Jeshua to this day — for she is the vision of the Goddess and she saw through everything that was "less than," that amazing and perfect Love. While she was not dedicated to the Temple as I was, she had been raised in a very pure and strict way to be prepared to be the Divine Mother incarnate and to be the mother of my beloved Jeshua.

She had been cared for, not sequestered, but shepherded. The biggest thing was her natural propensity. She just was the Light and so delicate and so pure, and yet so straightforward and willing to do the daily tasks and to build her friendships and to be the mother of her children and the wife of Joseph as well as holding the highest Light in the world for the embodiment of Jeshua as the Christ.

I feel like I am stumbling in my desire to express her purity and the joy I had in being with her and to show you her beauty, the radiance of her countenance. Everything about her was always shining. When she arrived that day and one of the acolytes came up to me, curtseyed (although we didn't call it that then) and said to me that she was here at the Temple, I was beside myself with joy. I ran across the garden and down the walk and to the gate. I threw it open and saw her standing there, the sky an azure blue with not a cloud and she, wrapped in her traditional blue headdress against the heat.

I leaped into her arms and she fell backwards laughing. There we sat together on the walkway. She laughed and laughed and held me and took my hands and kissed them and said, "Oh, Mary, you are such a breath of fresh air." I looked into her eyes and said, "I love you. You are my true mother." So this tells you of my relationship with Jeshua's sweet mother, that angelic presence who meant so much to me. It meant everything that she was there before the wedding to prepare me.

We did spend that day in preparation. She helped me break my fast and fed me special fruit and drinks, and bathed me in the ritual bath, combed my hair, dried my cheeks and took me through the order of my day that was very specific in the preparation to be the bride — for me, especially, as the bride of Christ.

That night we had a ritual of the whole Temple of women in the great open courtyard with an altar in the center under the stars with the full moon, all but the very fullest, hanging over us in the beautiful night sky. All my precious sisters came before me one by one, sat at my feet and offered me their blessings and spoke the words of their heart to me, of our friendship and our sharing and all the things they saw in their visions and the blessings of this marriage. They felt it deep in those realms beyond words.

I was honored, moved to tears and beyond the ability to speak. That night as I lay in bed I felt my Jeshua so powerfully with me that I could see his body before me. Though it shimmered in the moonlight, it was clear as if it were daylight. I wanted to reach out and touch him but I knew he wasn't corporeal. This was his spirit traveling to see me on the night before our wedding. I realized that we had promised we would see each other before we married in the Temple. This had not occurred because the Goddess had taken me in and walked me through her labyrinth of preparation for him.

I laughed in joy and said to him, "I am so glad you are here and I am ready to be your bride, my Jeshua, my Christ, and I am for you the Divine Feminine, the Goddess. I am ready to play my part." I know that he felt it. I could tell it in my bones and I knew that wherever he lay, we were together — not only in spirit but in the timeless truth of the world as well, beyond these seemingly solid structures of physical life. I felt the warmth of his Love. I felt his gentle hands caress me and I could hardly wait for the next day and our wedding.

*I choose the path that leads
straight into my heart
and feel the warm embrace of home.*

Chapter Fifteen

"...she could hold the Love that was required to be the bride of Christ..."

Mother Mary speaks:

Jeshua knew throughout his life that he was meant for one woman and that this woman was the other half of his soul. We spoke of this through many late nights and early mornings, even when he was very young. As he matured and began to feel the pull of that overlay of sexuality, we had many conversations about Divine Love-Making and he was firmly anchored in the reality of true and pure Love and he was ready.

Our life spans as human beings were much shorter then than yours are today, and so a woman matured at puberty and was married and began having children shortly after, at an age that you would consider still an adolescent. Women in our time and culture were mothers of families easily by fifteen years of age.

Jeshua, in his early twenties, was a deeply mature and very aware man who had a strength and presence and a vision that could span all philosophies, understand every human motivation, and stay totally connected to the voice of God within him. When he passed puberty, he began dreaming about his Mary and he would describe her to me in the mornings — hair as radiant as the morning sun and blazing like the sunset, eyes of emerald green and skin that he described as pearls shining in the moonlight.

I knew in my heart who it was, for I was friends with Mary's mother who was a woman dedicated in the Goddess Temple and whose life was given to the Goddess. But I believe for her it created a lack of maternal instinct and did create a separation between them. But little Mary was nurtured by hundreds of women and I was one of them. Whenever I saw her, and I saw her often for I also studied in the Goddess Temple — although I wasn't initiated, dedicated — I was very aware of the Divine Feminine of course, and the role that the feminine was to play in the Passion Play that was unfolding as the life of my Jeshua.

I held it in my heart in prayer and asked for every blessing upon them. But I didn't speak of it to Jeshua because I knew that a mother's Love can only go so far and he needed to hear the message from his heart when the Creator saw that the time was right. I held my own counsel and watched her grow and was filled with the greatest delight. I would laugh and say, "Oh, Goddess, God, You are so perfect!. Look what You are creating for my Jeshua...... She could not be a more perfect balance for him. Where he is studious, she is all laughter and action. Where he is philosophical, she is filled with impetuousness and the abandon that comes from perfect trust in You and in life. Life, Oh, Creator, she is so full of it that she will fill him up in ways only You can see, but I can feel it."

I watched her grow and did what I could to bridge her estrangement with her mother and her longing for a more nuclear family, for her father was a consort of the Goddess, meaning he also was dedicated in the Goddess Temple. Her birth was conceived in the highest of ritual. Her mother was a very esteemed High Priestess and her father was the true Love of her mother's life. But the culture of the Goddess didn't support the nuclear family but rather supported the community of worship with the Goddess at the pinnacle.

As the time came and Jeshua and Mary met as adults and fell in Love, my heart was singing with gladness. The closer the time came for this their public union — for of course they had already joined — I found the chorus of the Angels around me increasing continually, until I could hardly function for all the singing and joyous expression of cosmic Love that was pouring down from the Angelic realms and from the Masters. Of course, I was glad.

I arrived at the Temple of the Goddess the day before the wedding, feeling so excited, so uplifted with so much Love pouring through me that I was surprised I was corporeal at all — surprised that people could see me. I had to concentrate to be able to speak and to be understood for all the singing in the realms of Light.

Seeing Mary grounded me instantly and I knew that this is what she did for Jeshua. The richness of her spirit and the life bubbling in her, the joy of her smile and the vibrancy of her movements and the exuberance just poured forth from her, truly like a radiant sun. It washed my being in joy and brought me firmly into the celebration of life here now on Earth as it is in all the realms of God.

I dove in with all my heart in helping her prepare for the wedding. I spoke to her of all my wonderful memories of Jeshua and of the mischief that he would get into. I painted her pictures in words of the wonderful son who had grown into such an incredible man with depth and vision and grace, and such a connection to the Creator.

I could tell that she soaked it up and loved every moment. While she didn't seem particularly nervous, she did seem wound up, as you would say, full of so much energy she didn't know what to do with it. I set about helping her channel it and we began to sing the songs of the Goddess, to pray the prayers of purification for marriage. I prepared the ritual bath as the symbolic cleansing of the bride for the bridegroom. I combed her hair and oiled her skin and did all those things that a mother does for her daughter. We felt such joy in each other's presence and such a sense of camaraderie.

That night we joined with all the women. We anointed Mary with spikenard and aloes, and then surrounded her in the moonlight and spoke the names of the Goddess to her, telling her how we saw her as the Goddess of life in all of Her phases and faces, and Her perfect expression in her beloved daughter, Mary, the Magdalene.

Then she rose in her capacity as the Magdalene and led us in a ritual of acceptance where she chose with all her heart and will to accept the mantle of the embodied feminine Christ, the perfect counterpart for Jeshua. I couldn't hold back my tears. They poured from my eyes even while I smiled. They wet my gown all down the center. I felt so moved by the Goddess'

Love and Her presence before me as this beautiful woman, already my daughter in marriage, becoming the next day the daughter of my family and of my service to the world.

That night she too was shown the destiny that she had accepted when she came to Earth, shown all of it, every part, every bit, including Jeshua's death and resurrection. I asked her if she accepted. Of course, she said, "Yes." By this time it was midnight and there were very few women left. I could tell they were hand-picked by the Goddess for they were women who were wise and who could hold their counsel. We all knew it would be revealed only by the Creator, just who she is and what she had chosen to do on Earth.

And so it was that we lay down together in her room with the moonlight shining through the window and the hand of God as the feminine upon us. The night was full of the voices, not only of the Angels and their Love, but all of the Angels' servants who are the insects who sang that vibrational song, the OM, with us all through the night.

Mary dozed at times and woke again to walk the labyrinth of the Goddess and to pray and to pray and pray and to open her heart and to give herself in service to Jeshua and to give her heart to all they were meant to do. Every moment of that night was like spokes on a great wheel going out to touch another part of the world. Every song and prayer and open heart alive in the communion of The One was like the hub of that wheel, that radiant center pulsing outward through our hearts along the spokes to touch every Earth religion and begin to open them.

As the moon began to set, I took Mary to her bed and said, "It is time for you to sleep. Before you do, let me speak to you about the great dance of the Divine Masculine and Divine Feminine that I have been blessed to know so intimately and to share with my beloved Joseph." I spoke to her of Making Love between a man and a woman who were totally dedicated to The One, and I told her that even though she had shared much with Jeshua already, something miraculous would be happening that day, beginning with this wedding.

What it was I could only sense but I could feel its magnitude. I could feel its import for all of humankind. I also knew that I could trust God/Goddess Love to inform Mary and Jeshua in every moment, on every step of their road together. As dawn arrived and the sun began to crest over the hills, I said, "Mary, I have one last thing to share. That is the truth about Jeshua's birth and the power of his role in the world."

As I spoke, I could tell that Mary already knew everything I said — that she had received it all directly. I could see in her eyes that she already knew also what was coming. I was glad, because I knew that she was strong enough and open enough to be prepared and to be the rock upon which my beloved Jeshua stood as he brought a new era to the world. I knew that she, Mary, the Magdalene, could hold the Love that was required to be the bride of Christ.

I call out to the arms of God
that reach around the world,
and I settle into the living warmth
of the place nearest the divine heart
that gives life to mine.

Chapter Sixteen

"I trust the Creator in all things..."

Jeshua speaks:

The morning of our wedding dawned bright and clear. The sky was as blue as the Mediterranean. The first thing that I noticed was Nature's song, a great variety of voices of rejoicing. As I looked out of my window in the room I shared with Lazarus, I saw the Earth spirits dancing and I saw the great waves of the winds and I heard the wind spirits speak my name. Nature greeted me with joy on my wedding day.

I felt joy rising in me also and felt the presence of my beloved, my precious Mary. I spoke to her in my heart and said, "I greet you, dear. I come to you today as the holy bridegroom and I will worship at your feet." I dressed myself all in white and prepared my heart to accept my role as the incarnation of the energy of the Divine Masculine on Earth in a new way, with a deeper commitment and a statement for the world.

Feeling the call of the living presence of the great I AM that spoke within my spirit, soul and heart, I walked out of the village of Bethany and found a place in an olive grove to worship and to meditate. While the song of Nature swirled all about me and I heard the delightful chorus of insects humming, I sat in silence listening to that inner voice that spoke in stillness, as great as the living cosmos.

I was very surprised at what it had to say! I was shown a scene unfolding before my inner vision that drew my breath in, in a gasp, and made me hold it. What I saw was my arrival at the Temple in Jerusalem and the door shut in my face! Almost not believing what I was seeing, I turned to the Angels, those beloved friends and guides who had shared my way and guided me through every step of my Earthly life and whom I could hear clearly always. The Angels at times were able to show me how to relate to life in the world in a way that the presence of the living eternal God could not.

I called them to me and asked in humility for their assistance with what I had been shown. They verified that the Rabbis in the Temple in Jerusalem had made the decision to reject Mary Magdalene because she was an initiate of the Goddess and not a practicing Jew. At first I felt a sense of confusion, even outrage, and a little bit of panic, of course, because my wedding day had already dawned. It was here. Suddenly we had no Temple for the service and we had people coming, friends and family and all those whose lives they touched, people we could never notify in time, all of whom were going to show up at the great Temple of the Jewish faith in Jerusalem for our wedding.

I had felt so sure that this was where our wedding was meant to be, that this would be the beginning of our work, a statement in a larger way of where we stood in our dedication to the One. But as I sat and prayed and opened and listened to my heart, I began to understand that there was something deeper. What was happening this day, the day of my wedding in a very public way — a far more public way than the vows we took in the community of the Essenes — was actually the steps of the unfolding of history, the opening of the way of time. The path we trod this day would lay a path for God to bring balance to humankind of the masculine and the feminine in the world.

I still did not see how this was going to play out, and yet, play out I knew that it would. The first order of business was obviously my wedding day and telling my beloved, Mary, the Magdalene, about the new development as quickly as I could. So I said, "Beloved God, in whom I live and breathe, the living voice of Love that moves our being — move me this day and guide my every breath, my every word. Please guide my feet and take me to the place where I am to wed my beloved precious beautiful Mary Magdalene, she who is a part of my very being."

Deep within I heard the resounding "Yes" and was assured that I would be guided every step. I felt that great wash of the Creator's Love and I was bathed in His/Her blessing. As I breathed in this grace, I smelled lotus and lilies and rain and desert and mountain air. I breathed in the movement of God as living Love in the world and in every human being. Once again I saw before me the pattern of my life with Mary Magdalene and the great wheel of Light that we were bringing and the alignment of every star being and all the Love of God moving into this Cross of Creation that is the world appearing physical.

My whole being breathed a sigh of relief. I felt myself buoyed up on the winds of spirit and knew that I must go where the living spirit led, as usual. I rose from my meditation and thanked the olive trees, breathing in again the nectar of the Nature Spirits. I rushed into the house in Bethany of my beloved friends, Lazarus, Mary, Martha and their parents and thanked them with all my Love and deep appreciation for what they had given me. I told them what was happening. I asked them to pass the word to everyone they possibly could that the venue of our wedding was changing and that they should stay attuned to the voice they understood, that voice in which we all have communion, and I would let them know where to come.

"But, please," I said, "put on your wedding clothes and come into Jerusalem because there *will* be a wedding. This I promise you. Of this I am sure because my heart knows that this is our emergence as the great outpouring of living Love as the union of Divine Masculine and Divine Feminine in the world."

Then I ran as fast as my feet would carry me and lifted my vibration into the realms of Light, speaking to the electrons that made up the air that infused the life of Creation and the electrons that made my body. "I am the living wind, the movement of the spirit, and I am the heart of God in Jerusalem," I said to them. I became a living streak of Light, an arrow in the wind pointing to my beloved.

In a rush I was there. I spoke the words to bring the electrons back into the resonance of the physical. As I felt myself become grounded on the solid Earth, I knew the place for our wedding, just as surely as if a voice had spoken from the Heavens. With a great "Aha," and believe me, a breath of great relief, I realized that it was to be in the Goddess Temple. I saw how perfectly this made sense. I understood that the rejection of the Rabbis, of the Holy Ones of the Jewish Temple, did have to do with the masculine that had become tyrannical. We were birthing the new pattern of the unity of the Divine Masculine and Divine Feminine which I had seen played out in the realms of spirit as the preview for this life.

I saw the movement that would go from the Age of the masculine into the Age of the feminine as a step. Then, the life I Am with Mary Magdalene as the Twin Flame heart incarnated would bring the balance. Even if that balance did not come until another Age — this Age in which you now live — I knew we were walking the steps of the Creator's dance, even there that day.

I understood that I had to play out the scenario. I went to the Temple of the Jews and to the Sanctuary. As I raised my hand to knock upon the inner door, it opened. There was the Rabbi who had agreed to do our ceremony, to perform our union in public. I saw that behind him was a meeting of many members of the Sanhedrin, those austere leaders of Jewish law. Once again the voice within me said, "This is meant to be. It is the choice of life over the laws of the human mind."

I opened my mouth to speak and the Rabbi said to me, "Jeshua, we have made a decision, after much deliberation and holy prayers. All of us together are in agreement that this would not be the appropriate place for your wedding to Mary Magdalene because she is an initiate of the Goddess Temple." I looked him in the eye and prayed, "God, love him, and, Goddess, wrap him in Your forgiveness." I reached out and placed my hand on his forehead and sent the Light deep within and I watched as the seed of awakening took root in his heart.

Then I said to him further, "I understand and I honor this, for I trust the Creator in all things, and even though you tell me this on my wedding day, I know that my every step is led by Him, blessed by Her. I go with a joyful heart and I give you blessings, all of you. We will speak together many times, and by the way, all of you are welcome at our wedding wherever it is held today."

As I left, I acknowledged that I could say no more because even though my inner voice had shown me the venue, I still did not know if those who held the Creator's Will as the Goddess in the world would agree. In other words, I had to go to the High Priestess of the Goddess Temple and of course I had to go to my beloved.

This time I walked, but I walked quickly across the dusty streets of Jerusalem, weaving in and out between the stalls of goods, the donkey carts and the crowds of men. As quickly as I could I made it to the gate of the beautiful Temple of the Goddess. As I stood at the gate I acknowledged the difference in the two buildings. The Temple of the Jews was very grand. The great dome shone gold to impress the minds of men and there were vast and intricate courtyards and much discourse on the laws of the Torah, as well as the courtyard of the sacrifice. I will not go into this now.

What I saw as I stood before the gate of the Temple of the living God in the form of the Divine Feminine was the soft and unassuming architecture of the Temple and the very welcoming vibration. The gate was covered with vines full of grapes not yet ripened, and there were plants and trees peeping over the wall. Everywhere I looked there was color and sweetness and the symbols of life.

When the gate opened, the Priestess who greeted me bowed and said, "The High Priestess is expecting you but not yet your beloved — at least I don't think that she knows you are here. Who would you like to see first?" She smiled at me with such warmth with a twinkle in her eye, and her smile made a great dimple show in her cheek. I laughed and took her hand and said, "Thank you for your warmth and for this wonderful greeting. I greet you as well in Her name. I would like to see my beloved Mary, the Magdalene."

"Of course," she said, laughing, and turned to lead the way. I noticed her beautiful hair like a shimmering waterfall all the way down her back. Everything about her was a song to life and I knew that this was right, that this was the right place. With purpose and assurance that all was unfolding as it should, I went to see my beloved.

When I arrived, Mary was sitting in a beautiful room. There were couches all along the wall. Actually a better description would be cushioned benches, just to give you the image. She rose and came to me and leaped into my arms, and we kissed passionately, for quite some time I might say. When I finally was able to pull myself away, it was all I could do to catch my breath. "Oh, my beloved Mary, how I love you with all my being and how I have longed every moment to be with you, even though I know we are ever with each other in the spirit. Our every breath and heartbeat is shared, but I still have longed to touch your hand and see your face and hear your beautiful melodious words." Then I ran out of language and just stood in awe of her.

As we walked to the door, the sunlight touched her hair and she became totally radiant. The light within and the light of the sun met and blended and all I could see was pure beauty, as Light, as color and as the movement of form. But Mary was always fluid and I felt deep within this movement of hers that was/is like the tide in the ocean. That became the soothing rhythm that spoke to my being of Love and of my place with her.

Words are so inadequate, for this Love we share is still as explosive now as it was then and the passion between us, the power of this Love and its beauty that can just overwhelm my whole being was certainly present that day. Somehow I gathered enough of my wits to say to her, "Mary, we have a situation." Now all of you who have experienced a wedding day understand these words and you understand the effect. Suddenly she stopped, backed up and went, "Oh, Jeshua, no, tell me what is happening."

I could see her eyes were wide and she was holding her breath just as I had done when I realized we were in for big changes this day. I was able to take her hands and say, "Sweet Mary, relax. It is all part of the divine plan. So let's go outside and sit on the Goddess bench and listen to the divine fountain and I will tell you what is happening."

When I explained what had happened, at first she also felt some outrage at being rejected by the Rabbis. But when I told her all I had learned about the pattern of life and what we were creating that day and that the spirit of Love had guided me here for our wedding in the Temple of the Goddess, she was overjoyed. Of course, this was her spiritual home and this is as yet her gift to the world — to be this embodiment (for lack of a better word) of the great Divine Feminine and to let it live and speak through her. She was also to give that gift to me of the rich life of that continual movement of Love that was the ground of her being and that from which she always moved.

The Temple of the Goddess was already dedicated to Love and acknowledged the Divine Masculine and the Divine Feminine, and also acknowledged the sacred union of Love through the body and into the spirit. The Temple even had the rituals of holiness in which to express it. I knew once again that this was right. So, together, hand in hand we went to see the Priestess, what you could call the Great Magdalene, she who had earned the highest honor of the embodiment on Earth of the Divine Feminine.

We knocked on her door together and waited. She opened the door herself and invited us in. She was as yet very beautiful, though much older than we were. When we came in and both of us tried to speak at once, she laughed and said, "I know why you are here because She has told me, that voice of the Goddess in whom I live, by which I breathe. She came to me this morning and showed me that we are to be honored to host this union of the ones who serve the Christos embodied for the world, and Her servant, our Mary." We turned to each other and smiled. Then we turned back to her and said, "Revered High Priestess, we thank you and we would like to honor your rituals. Yet we also have things we have need to say to each other." She said, "Of course."

I knew that from that moment Mary and I would not be parted. We were on Earth to be this living whole of Love — the braid of God, Divine Masculine, Divine Feminine and the living God, interwoven together so tightly that that braid could not come undone. It is the braid of life.

We returned to my beloved's room that she had been given for her time in the Temple. It waited for her whenever she was called to return and perform her duties as a Magdalene. Together we began to get ready. Suddenly I realized we had to spread the word. Everything was working as it should, but what about our guests? So hand-in-hand we ran back across Jerusalem, dust flying up from our feet and onto my perfect wedding clothes. All I could do was laugh as I felt the exhilaration and I felt the living God lifting our hearts and giving them wing.

I could almost see the heart we shared as one, one heart beating but with two wings of the spirit, wings that at that very moment were lifting us higher and higher into ecstasy. We arrived breathless at the Holy Temple and ran through the courtyard. I waved at many of those revered scholars with whom I had had many a debate. We asked each Rabbi and every man who served in the Temple if they would be willing to tell our guests that we were being married at the Temple of the Goddess.

Some of them resisted, but most said, "Yes." Then we were told we could have a crier at the Temple entrance, someone who would make the announcement continually as much as he could — the announcement that the wedding of Jeshua Ben Joseph and Mary the Magdalene was now to be held at the Goddess Temple. But who were we going to find?

Once again the search was on for the perfect solution. Then I saw a young man whom I had befriended many times when I had come to the Temple to enjoy the debate with many of the Rabbis and scholars. We enlisted the help of this young man who was getting ready for his Bar Mitzvah, entering into the community of Jewish men. I had been assisting him with his studies of the Torah and with his deeper understanding of the spirit.

He happily agreed to be our crier and to announce regularly the change in our wedding. We thanked him and hugged him and left him to do his work and ran back to the Temple of the Goddess. If you could have seen Jerusalem in that day you would understand how different it looked from anything that you can imagine. The streets were filled not only with dust but with camel dung and the excrement of many donkeys and even some horses and the remnants of food and hay and many other things. I was running in bare feet. But again, all I could do was laugh. Feet are easy to wash, I thought.

We taste the sweetness
of who we truly are,
and the overwhelming response
is to want to share it
with another
and another and another.

Chapter Seventeen

"I had forgotten my humanity, the brothers and sisters I was here to serve..."

Jeshua speaks:

We rushed up the walkway to the Temple of the Goddess, that beautiful oasis on the edge of Jerusalem. But at the entrance, my heart stood still and I stood rooted to the spot. Suddenly my consciousness expanded, leaping free of every boundary and I found myself in winging, singing communion with the living breathing One that we name God. My beloved Mary — so attuned to me — saw that I was held suspended in a moment of sudden divine communion and inner vision, and she allowed me my space and silence.

With the vision that has no limits, I saw all the Love, the hope and the upliftment out of fear that was meant to come through me and Mary, the Magdalene. I saw how it funneled through the heart we are together into the world, bridging every opposite and every difference, bridging the illusion of space and time and bridging also the masculine and the feminine, creating the merging with God.

With this expanded knowledge, I knew immediately that what I had seen and thought about our wedding had been too limited. I had been focused on me, and Mary, my beloved, and for a moment I had forgotten my humanity, the brothers and sisters I was here to serve. I stood in shock over gaining this awareness. I realized that, even in the throes of our great Love, I had never before forgotten for even a moment what our true mission was. In that same moment of reckoning, the voice of the living spirit spoke within me and said to me, "This is your learning, dearest Jeshua — to see how humanity sees."

A pattern began for me this day — moments of forgetting who I am and why I came — just moments where my attention was focused on myself or on me and Mary. Some of you have had the experience of taking wing and coming free of the illusion of time for moments or for hours, but then becoming enmeshed in the world again. For me it was the other way.

My whole life I had been alive to the singing universe and every breath I breathed was in harmony with The One. So for me these moments of forgetting were a shock and a revelation. I felt a deepening of my tender Love and my compassion for humankind for I could not imagine living as humanity did and as yet does — disconnected from that living glory and that singing awareness.

Even in the midst of these revelations and these changes that had been happening so fast and furious, I felt the hand of God, the Creator, upon me and felt the movement of the Goddess beneath my feet. I found myself the meeting place for the two. I knew that the hand of destiny was upon me and upon this my wedding day.

I took a breath and said within, "Beloved God, I am yours. Do with me what you will." In that moment of communion I understood that this day and the pattern it wove for the future had barely begun, and with a laugh, I said, "I am ready. Show me."

I realized that in my moment of forgetting, my narrow vision hadn't taken into account all the feelings and the thought forms of those I serve with the symbol of this wedding. I recognized instantly that it could not be held in the Temple of the Goddess any more than it could be held in the Temple of the Jews in Jerusalem. This was a time of great divisiveness, especially in that place that you now call the Holy Land.

There was the Roman influence with its paean of gods and goddesses. There were the Jews with their fierce determination for the One God, but who were beginning to name God masculine. There was the deeply rooted culture of the Goddess that had been with humankind for many Ages. This was born of the understanding that came unspoken through the Earth and into the blood and bones that life was a living glorious and intelligent thing, the living spirit imbuing all of it. The most accessible to humanity was the feminine, the Great Mother, the Goddess.

At the time when I lived in Galilee and this time of my wedding in Jerusalem, the Goddess was still the most prevalent form of worship. And yet, those who had rejected our wedding in the Jewish Temple would certainly not set foot in the Temple dedicated to Shekinah, the Goddess, the feminine spirit.

I realized in that moment of communion that the path this wedding had taken today, my wedding day, had to go one step further in creating this pattern for humanity. It had to be the coming together of the masculine and feminine just as is my Love with Mary and that it must include every person, no matter the form of worship or the aspect of The One to which they prayed.

In that moment, my reverie was interrupted as the door to the Temple opened and there stood my mother. She was radiant as always, her beauty taking my breath away as it always did. There was instant communion between us. I felt a great freedom from her eyes as they sparkled and from her voice as she laughed. She held out her arms to me and to my Mary, who had stepped to one side, silently waiting for me to give her a signal that my inner communion was complete.

Both of us rushed into her arms. Letting out a breath, I said, "Oh, my mother…" "Don't worry," she said, soothingly. "It is done." I turned to Mary, my beloved, and started to explain what I had just received in my inner vision — that our wedding day was about to undergo yet another change. But I saw immediately in her eyes that my Mary had already grasped that another shift was occurring. She laughed and looking into my mother's eyes, she said, "Well, tell us! What is the plan now?"

This was a day of many revelations and shocking change as the day of our wedding careened back and forth. For those of you who live in a modern reality, this may seem unbearable, but it actually was not that unusual, living as we did. Without means of communication other than messengers and our own feet, we often found ourselves creating gatherings, even important ones on a moment's notice.

Then, the front gate to the Temple courtyard opened and there was my beloved friend, Joseph of Arimathea joining us on the walkway. Always so full of life, he threw back his head and gave a great and deep belly laugh and said, "Oh, Jeshua. What would you do without me?" Then he laughed again. We all walked into the inner courtyard and sat together on a bench, while Joseph and my mother began to inform us of what had been arranged and what we were to do.

Rather than go into every detail here, for I have shared enough, I will tell you that the solution was elegant and they had already accomplished almost all of it except for communicating with our crier and changing his message. The wedding venue had become the great outdoors! This felt so perfect to both of us. There was a beautiful hill right above the Goddess Temple that wasn't part of the Temple property. Rather it was a part of the City of Jerusalem, although it wasn't tended like a garden.

I could feel the song of Nature as she welcomed us and told me this had been the plan all along — that we would be completely available to all who wanted to come and we would be out under the stars. Our wedding time was planned for the setting of the sun with the ceremony to begin just before it. This way we could celebrate with the moon and the stars as people had always done.

My heart rejoiced at the perfection. But what about the blending of the two ways? My mother proceeded to tell me that she had arranged it all. Our dear old family friend, an elderly Rabbi who had come to witness the wedding, would now be performing it, with the assistance of the High Priestess and with the blessings of any other officiant who felt moved to participate. Mary was elated and said to me, "Oh, my feet are ready to dance, my Jeshua. I am so excited about our wedding and I would marry you every day. I am so glad that She has brought me to you and that He blesses our union."

And so it was settled in a way that felt perfect, and created this merging of the pathways of worship into one celebration that included all whose hearts told them to join. It had already been arranged by Joseph and my mother, in cooperation with the Goddess Temple, that the kitchens would be at our disposal. A cadre of women was ready to help. The cooking had begun. Joseph had arranged for a great canopy to be erected on the side of the top of the hill so that there would be shelter for the food and the wine. Plenty of open space remained for the ceremony and for dancing. Everything that was going to be present originally would simply be present out under the sky. I was filled with joy.

Mother Mary speaks:

During the week before Jeshua's wedding, all I could do was sit in my sacred room by my altar and listen to the Angels' song and watch the patterns unfolding, seeing the blossoming of Jesus and Mary's Love and seeing also what would come of it in the form of a beautiful granddaughter. But I knew that that was in the future.

I saw also the great sacrifice as Jeshua became the bridge, bridging the terrible separation between humanity and the Creator and making a pathway Home for everyone. I knew what it meant and always have, and as I said, this was not the first time that we had done this. It was the time that applied to your Age and most of you were there with me and you remember.

As I prayed and I listened and I sang with the Angels and I communed with my special Archangel Gabriel, I entered the silence and I looked. What I saw was the unfolding of the Ages and how the emphasis would change. First the masculine becoming dominant through the Jewish lineage, and then a swing back to the awareness of the Goddess in a backlash to the other. Then, there was the coming to the center with the awareness of Twin Flame Love and the perfect balance of both the feminine and the masculine in each and every heart.

I came to recognize that the wedding could not be in the Jewish Temple. I could feel the unrest building there and I had always understood that Jeshua made them nervous. Now I felt that they were scared. I already understood how the minds that had succumbed to fear in the Jewish tradition were becoming calcified and the law was taking precedence over Love.

When I opened to my Goddess and I listened, I heard many women's voices singing in a ritual of marriage and dedication with which I was familiar. I realized that the Goddess Temple might become the place for the marriage, because it was much more in line with the freedom and flexibility that was Jeshua's life and that had to be present to embrace this great energy that is Jesus and Mary.

In the Temple of the Goddess, life was still worshiped in the highest place and the awakening to the Goddess in every moment. There was more room to embrace the Twin Flames of Jeshua and Mary Magdalene and to support who they are, and to point the arrow of destiny all the way to your Age. In your Age would come the re-establishment of the fullness of the Creator's Love as the Divine Feminine as well as the Divine Masculine and the transcendence, then, of both as one great Love that fuels the cosmos.

Yet, I knew that there were many who would not be comfortable in the Temple of Women. I knew that the marriage would unfold as it was meant to, and gave myself over to attunement with the movements of spirit within time. I felt a great rush of blessing from the Angels, and a vision of the marriage of my Jeshua and his Mary came before me. I was shown the magnificent solution, beyond all temples and containment. I was called to make the arrangements for the wedding in the glorious temple of Nature, on the gracious hilltop beyond the Goddess Temple, beneath the moon and the stars. Every detail came into its place effortlessly and I felt in my heart the rightness of this final location.

When Joseph of Arimathea and I communicated the news to Jeshua and Mary, their boundless joy and excitement was the answer to my prayer. The public wedding of my Jeshua and his Mary was open to the world, as were their hearts.

May you know the heart and soul
of the Beloved within me
is known in the
Oneness
of the heart and soul
of the Beloved
within you.

Chapter Eighteen

"...holding the Light of the Christos and the torch given to us for humanity..."

Jeshua speaks:

With light hearts and filled with joy over the new arrangements for our wedding, Mary and I went into a Chapel of which there were many in the Goddess Temple complex. This one was small and beautiful and filled with oil lamps. The altar held an eternal flame. As with all of the altars of the Goddess it was overflowing with the symbols of abundant life — with flowers and with fruit.

We sank to our knees together, held hands and bowed our heads, and went into the silence, opening our hearts to God. Our experience was the receiving of blessings far beyond that of our human life — the blessings of holding the Light of the Christos and the torch given to us for humanity of an expanding vision of service, of giving and of joy.

We accepted that torch in humility and accepted the beginning of our outer mission — that which we were born into the world to bring. While this was seven years earlier than what is today considered the beginning of my ministry, it was the beginning of the movement of our life together outward into the world, joining the many religions, the many perspectives and forms of worship into one great wheel of Light for humanity.

This was the thrust of our travels to which we had committed after the wedding. We were shown the pattern continually and shown how it evolved as humanity changed. We knew how this weaving together of all of the pathways to God would bring us full circle, home to Galilee and to that final building of the bridge.

But this day was a day of beginnings, a day that had already contained many days-worth of exciting changes and also of the unfolding Love between me and my beloved. As I opened my eyes, she opened hers and we turned from the altar to each other. I gazed into those eyes of sparkling green and I fell right into her heart.

I knew the great Love of the Divine Feminine, as She wraps and supports us all, had come to me in this beautiful form of my beloved Mary, the Magdalene of this Temple and my Twin Flame. Our hearts leaped into glorious ecstatic communion. We rose in the spirit, into communion with the living, moving, ever-breathing, joyous, unending ecstasy of our holy and infinite union and our worship of the Creator, together as one, as one Love, as one heart, as one being in the truth.

Eventually we returned to the focus of the Chapel, our bodies vibrating with the power of the Light. We knew it was time to get ready — that the time of the ceremony was getting close. I touched her face and caressed her cheeks and brushed a gentle kiss across her lips. Then I placed my hands upon her heart and said with all my being, "Mary, I Am yours. You are the heart of me. I am honored to marry you this day and every day with my heart, with my intention and in any kind of ceremony that you would like." She laughed and threw her arms around me. We held that embrace for a long time and only reluctantly pulled apart, each of us to go and get dressed in a separate space, not to see each other again until the wedding.

For most of the people who would be our witnesses this day, this was a brand new marriage between us, for the community of the Essenes was very quiet, in some ways secretive, and very few understood them. It wasn't common knowledge that we were already joined. This was perfect because this day was for symbolism and for service and not for us. This was now imprinted on my heart by the Great Beloved, the I AM, and I was humbled and grateful.

It came at last, the time for our public wedding. As I emerged from the room I had been given in which to prepare, I found myself surrounded by women of every shape and size and dressed in every color that you could possibly imagine. I thought of all the colors of Nature and how spectacular the Creator is in giving us all these symbols of beauty and naming them the Feminine.

I smiled in the greatest Love for every one of them and let myself enjoy being tended and pampered and fussed over and very carefully herded to my wedding. I emerged from the Temple into the daylight that was fading. The day was just as beautiful as it had been from its dawning. The sky was tinged with the beginnings of the sunset, painted in pinks and lavenders. To my surprise there were streams of people coming, all of them headed for the hill, all of them coming to our wedding. I stood still, taking it in. I was very surprised, especially with all of the changes that had happened that day. I began to wonder if everyone was going to fit, even though the hill was quite large and the top of it quite flat. It had been used for ceremonies for ages. But this was a lot of people!

I quickly said a prayer and asked my beloved God to make room for everyone easily and to let every person hear what the ceremony truly meant — let them hear it with their hearts and spirits. My prayer didn't last long because I was pushed forward by all the women who were so lovingly attending me. I was dressed in white as we were meant to be. This, too, of course, was a symbol. While my feet were shod with sandals, it was my intention to be barefoot for the wedding so that I could feel the life of the Earth beneath me as I felt the breath of the spirit in the wind and as I felt the presence of the Creator's Love in constant communion in my heart.

And so I went to meet my bride. An altar had been created and upon it there were symbols of all religions. I knew that this was the hand of my mother for she was always in perfect communion with God and she too understood the meaning of symbols and the pattern we were weaving this day. Before the altar stood my beloved Mary. She was radiant. My heart almost stopped beating and I could hardly breathe for her beauty. Her hair was done in braids that circled around her head with some of it still falling loose down her back. Through every braid was woven flowers and greenery. She looked to me truly like the Goddess, standing in a dress of white filled with embroidery from the hands of many women, some of whom had even sewn on it that day.

Around her shoulders was a scarf of many colors, what you would call, I believe, a shawl. It was luminous in the evening Light. I could see the pulse of her heart beating as she breathlessly awaited me, her bridegroom. All of a sudden I was thrown into the consciousness of the cosmos and the arrow of Light pierced me. I heard within me, "The bridegroom is the Christos."

As I stood before my people and looked out upon that sea of faces, I felt my heart according the truth of the I AM that is ever such a living part of me. I felt the merging of all these songs of myself into the living melody of the Creator, moving forth as the energy of the living heart that I Am. I understood that all of us together are this song of many parts, woven into a beautiful symphony of the Creator loving as us in every imaginable way.

I felt the shared breath and with the vision of God alive in me, I could see the life energy of everyone present merging into a great wheel of Light and substance that became an opening, a swirling vortex, a doorway to the Creator, intimately present in humanity. At last it overflowed from heart and mouth, and I spoke to my beloved of the great I AM within us. I told her that my Love for her was truly limitless and timeless for I acknowledged that we are one with the endless Love of our Creator, and the power of God resided in me. The Love of God as feminine bloomed as Mary. As we joined in that glorious unity, we spoke forth God's promise to lift each heart into communion with the mystery and the grace that surrounds us and brings us forth into joy.

My awareness of the singing endless harmony of the multi-layered movement of timeless Love became woven into a greater song of devotion and sharing as the spirit opened and lifted every heart present. Our wedding became a time of holy witness to the power of the spirit to join all hearts and to open wide the vision of every person to his/her place in the glorious dance of Love that is the world. As I watched, I could see with the vision of my heart each heart present come alive and become luminous. I felt the vibration rising and with it, the inspiration as each person present felt the living hologram, felt the kiss of the endless mystery of which they are part, and felt the power of our hearts united.

The Priestess came to stand in front of Mary, the symbol of the feminine, and the old Rabbi stood in front of me as each one spoke in turn of marriage, of holiness and creating a household for God. Together we agreed. Then we faced each other just as the sun truly set and went down beyond the horizon. The colors came up radiant, painted in celebration by Nature moving at the hand of God. Great rays of Light of every color of the rainbow shot forth from the horizon across the sky in a great arc of Light. The birds came two by two to celebrate our Love. The bees buzzed around our heads, even though it was twilight, and I heard the chorus of the nightingales, but also of the insects and of the movement of the Devas. Every voice said, "Yes. It is done." Then every voice said, "It has begun." Then every voice began to sing as together the Priestess and the Rabbi spoke the words of holy union and pronounced us husband and wife.

A great roar of appreciation thundered through the crowd as all of them stomped their feet and clapped their hands and shouted our names. I drew Mary to me in a passionate kiss as we were showered with Light. Everything dissolved into pure energy as once again I fell into her eyes and we merged, our spirits as one, our hearts sharing one heartbeat. Deep within us we held the knowledge of what it was that had begun this day.

Both of us knew that our Love was truly timeless, that we were and are together for all eternity but that this life that we had agreed to live in the world was a life of public scrutiny and great service and we knew that it would take every bit of our dedication. We gave it, as once again we said "Yes" to the Creator's Love and "Yes" to what we came into the world to bring. "Yes" also to the great blazing Light that is the joining of the masculine and the feminine.

Someone brought the cup for me to stomp in the Jewish tradition and someone brought the Chalice for us to drink from together in the tradition of the Goddess. Our beloved friends and family gave us their blessings as one after another came forth to say their accolades. All sang the praises of this wedding and this day, and said their thanks to God, the living universe for all our blessings.

The crowd thinned a little bit as the sun went down, but the number of people still surprised me. As I looked around I saw so many faces that beheld the

Light, that came from my joining with Mary the Magdalene. All that she held as the Goddess within her and all that I held as the Christos was joined in a great pattern of Light that evening and dedicated to humanity.

We began to dance and to celebrate. We danced the *hora* under the stars. There was a great circle of human beings, those who worshiped the Goddess, those who worshiped God and those who worshiped many gods and goddesses and we all celebrated together. We danced the dances of the Jewish people. We danced the dances of the Romans, and we danced the great snake dance of the Goddess which was so much fun.

I felt a vibration of harmony moving through the crowd. The soft Light that comes when hearts are open infused everyone. The beauty of the moon as it hung in the sky, so big and full... the velvet softness of the night all around the hill... The dancing flickering of the torch lights around us... the cornucopia of all the food...all the flowers on the altar... and the headiness of the wine... I saw it all with the eyes of the living spirit. I saw how it can be for humankind as each one joins hearts in a celebration of life, this circle of harmony.

I felt within me a deep contentment, even as I heard once again, "It is begun."

Mary Magdalene speaks:

How can I even begin to describe this wedding day? Even with all the chaos and changes, it became for me the epitome of a life of beauty and a dedication to Jeshua and to the people whom we love. Every moment of our wedding was so filled with portent, with the great movement of spiritual tides, with the power and the purpose of the very Heavens and all the blessings of the Earth. Not to mention the joyous support of the people who came together to bridge all their differences and to celebrate our Love.

The stars that night were blazing with a greater Light than ever seen before on Earth. I was not the only one who saw it. People who would ordinarily not notice such things found their eyes drawn upward, as they witnessed that Light. As we danced in the torch light under the moon, it was as if every person's breath was singing the great OM together and the harmony was picked up by the Angels and they became our chorus. All the spirits of Nature were our rhythm section as we danced the dance of life.

I felt the movement of the Goddess within me rising through my body and filling my being with the timeless fertility of life in which we bring forth Her blessing, bringing our consciousness into artistic creation in worship of Her. Whether this creation is worlds or paintings or music of the spheres, it is all our deepest form of worship, that which we create for Her.

I knew that the altar of my Love with Jeshua was going to be one that required sacrifice but also that was overflowing with such beauty that every moment was worship. I let my heart flow free with abandon that night. I danced and sang and let the spirit move my feet, and I certainly wore my heart out there for all to see whenever I gazed on my beloved Jeshua. I felt that timeless rising of the energy of divine sexuality within us, the ageless celebration of life's movements through the masculine and the feminine.

The Goddess culture or religion had always worshiped openly that powerful union that is Love-Making and celebrated the coming together of men and women as a form of worship of the Goddess. Our worship always included the beauty of Nature and the overflowing gratitude for life, for the power of symbols to enhance our creative power and our life blood and fertility.

I put all that I am into expressing that energy. When I looked into my Jeshua's eyes, we ignited and I could feel the passion within us rising and our energies entwining. Every touch of our hands was totally sensuous, not just physical but an interweaving of energies, for we were always aware of that greater scope of our lives and of the illusion of the physical.

Especially for me in being the mate of Jeshua, a man blazing with God's Light — to touch him was to know the miracle of the movement of Light and energy. I knew that even though he was "incarnated," he was never fully physical and never anchored into this world as others were, and as I had chosen to be. Sometimes when I would touch him, it was like touching a beam of sunlight. I could feel the heat and pulse and the energy that he was, but it seemed as if my hands just moved right through him. And yet, the passion was always there, passion that tingled through my body, my being, my very atoms and certainly ignited my heart.

We danced and sang with our hearts completely open. As our eyes locked and we looked out at all the people, the Love we felt together was deep and powerful, poignant and beautiful, and it was all for them. Each precious person, old or young, large or small, each one carried that spark of God, and each one labored to make his/her life useful and worthwhile. Some of them had very difficult lives and we honored them immensely and always did whatever we could to assist them in any way possible.

This night I knew that the greatest gift we could give was to bring people into our joy and to let them release the world for a little while and dance in the fields of God. We did this, weaving our magic through them. I wove the Love of the great Goddess and Jeshua brought down the Light of the Christ, until the whole hilltop and all the people on it were lit from within. Everyone felt the night was magical, and they felt the Creator's blessing on them personally, as well as on us.

Then, at last, about four in the morning, as you reckon time, the last stragglers left, including our families who kissed us and gave us their blessings and looked at us with those secret smiles. They knew what dance of the Goddess we would be celebrating! At last I was there with my beloved, my Jeshua, on the hilltop alone under the stars. Even though we were in the heart of Jerusalem and not far from the Temple, we knew that everyone there would give us wide berth and honor this sacred time for us.

For us and for those who worshiped the Goddess, there is no greater setting than Nature as a backdrop for Love-Making, for Nature celebrates the joy of the holy communion of man and woman, Divine Masculine and Divine Feminine, that honors the movement of the great Creator in His/Her explosion into fully conscious life.

That night we came to each other, laying down a blanket that we had tucked away for just this time, and in the soft whisper of a summer breeze, we met each other, completely naked in heart, body, soul and spirit. As we joined, we were lifted into a greater experience of glory, a pinnacle untouched before, even in all the beauty we shared. We exploded together into a great expansion of shooting stars, and living lights and the Creator's magnificence, and shot upward, our spirits glowing and our hearts one great fire, into the glory of Creation itself. We became One with the living cosmos and One with that great eternal merging that brings forth all created life.

Something quickened within us in that moment that was greater than a human conception. It was the birth of a Love for humanity that brought God/Goddess even closer and impregnated the world with the Creator's Love more deeply than it had ever been. A living magnet was created within every heart, every atom and electron, that would allow God to pull humanity back Home to Love.

As we became the vessels for this mystery, our hearts accorded it within us and within our marriage as the essence of who we are together and what we are here to bring — the gift of freedom from the separation from God. We then slept in each other's arms, wrapped in that blanket on the firm and somewhat rocky ground. I felt only Jeshua, his heartbeat and his breath living within me. I felt my ear upon his chest, and the rhythm of his heart was my lullaby. I slept deeply beyond any dream, simply floating in his Love

Awaken our spirits flowing from
Your divine spirit,
spiraling and touching the Earth
and opening the bridge
that connects all worlds to
the Kingdom of You.

Chapter Nineteen

"I became a new man, just washed in the gift of Mary Magdalene and speechless with gratitude."

Jeshua speaks:

On the morning after our public wedding, our celebration of our Love, I awoke to find the whole world changed. Even before I opened my eyes, I knew that I was different and that everything I experienced of life would not ever be the same. I reached out and touched my beloved and felt the silky softness of her skin and the rising of the great flame of our Love and my desire for her — for her as Mary and for her as the Divine Feminine aspect of God.

I understood that it was this merging with that which she gave to me through her own soul, her spirit, that had enriched my life so totally that I was a different person. When I opened my eyes, all that I saw confirmed it, for the world that I saw that morning was stunningly beautiful. The colors were drenched with a richness that I had never seen before. The vibrancy of life in the world was absolutely holy and I bent my head in awe and said, "Thank You, God, for these things, for the new sight I have been given by Your gift of my beloved and the beginning of our work."

As I turned and looked into my Mary's eyes, I felt Heaven returning to me in a way that I didn't even know was missing, and returning to the Earth and humanity. It was anchored through her glorious heart and her deep acceptance of her divinity as the incarnation of the Goddess of Divine Feminine Love. I knew that she stood for God as the feminine and would stand so for centuries of women, and that it would be her life upon which the world would turn back into unity at the closing of the Ages, that time which is now.

In my instant comprehension of all this powerful shifting, I recognized truly the gift that I had been granted. I saw that of myself, I had not been fulfilled, even though my life was truly numinous and everywhere I looked I saw Light and everything I heard was God. But the depth and the richness of my soul had been missing without her, and life in the world became such a blessing as only the feminine can reveal it — making every object a jewel in the necklace of the Goddess and every person a priceless gem in the splendor of Her heart.

Hands joined, we fused, looking deep into each other, hearts taking wing once again. We sang our prayers to the Light of a new day and to the dawning of our work. Everything around us was also singing. Nature heralded our union. The dedication of our hearts was truly complete. The movement of the feminine within me returned me to my original design as part of that glorious dual flame that worships at the altar of God and forms the pattern of the cosmic DNA that is the basis for all things.

This reclamation of Real Love brings the physical world back to the center and restores every life stream, every consciousness and every heart to its true inheritance as the beautiful expression of God. I saw how the feminine brought the Earth back to life and restored its true vibration. It literally unlocked the prison of physicality and body and restored the holy energy of the movement of God's Love to that which we named the world.

When the world returned to me as a richer, deeper, fulfilled consciousness, I recognized the balance that Real Love brings. It grants to all the world, and of course to humanity, true centeredness and divinity. Real Love brings all of life back to joy in the sacred and glorious moment in which we love and live. Everything my heart saw of the world with my heart's perception was a living moving breathing song to the Goddess, She who caresses and holds all things in the most tender Love and dedication, the Divine Mother making all things right.

In my simple way, I try to express to you now the power of the Twin Flame heart and its restoration of the world to its true divinity and to the original cause which is the expression of the beauty and divinity of God's creative heart. That heart is you and me and all that we are created to be as the luminous conduits of God's Creation that express through us right now as the world.

I say to you, to all of you, that this great and moving Love is also yours. This is the time in the turning of the Ages, the time when the gate of time opens and you are meant to be free. The key to the lock on this gate is Real Love, the Love of true Twin Flames. The dispensation has been given to draw together these hearts and to bring them forth in service to the awakening of humanity and the return of the world to the Eden that is its Real identity.

As I watched Mary on that morning after our wedding, the sun was well up. The sunlight of late morning blended with her hair and created a rainbow of all the colors of fire, molten and magnificent, sparkling like her crown, the crown of the Goddess she is. As she saw me admiring her, there was a flash of shyness and humility, and then I saw her literally "put on" the Goddess. I saw her remember what we had shared and recognize that something had also been granted to her in our Love. After lifting to the very pinnacle of Love and sharing it with someone so perfectly beyond anything I had ever dreamed or imagined, I have to tell you I honestly wanted to worship at her feet and simply follow her around day after day telling her of her beauty and her power.

But then she laughed at me as only Mary could do and said, "Oh, Jeshua, aren't we a pair? We have certainly been hit by a new reality that has knocked us over with Love. But we must remember life's simplicity and the holiness of the day-to-day — that the Goddess is truly in the little things by which we live. So come, my Jeshua, and dance with me now in the garden of our Love. I want to see the sunlight playing tag with us and see it showing me the radiance of you."

Then she kissed me and I was lost once again in the vastness and the great ecstasy of our Love, as with shivers and tremors I became what you would call "putty" in her hands and just breathed then into her hair and said, "I love you."

She rose and pulled me up and went running across the hilltop, laughing every step of the way. She turned to me and said, "Jeshua, catch me!" and dashed away instantly. And so we laughed just like children in the morning sunlight, and I became a new man, just washed in the gift of Mary Magdalene and speechless with gratitude. When, breathless, we stopped playing, I laughed and said, "Mary, you are the fountain of the Goddess and I am so privileged to drink from you. Now shall we take this amazing Love, this elixir of God's Light and take it outward to humanity, and let it be for everyone a blessing as it is for us?"

Mary's eyes turned more serious and she took my hand and she said, "Yes, of course. I have seen this journey upon which we embark today and I have seen the web of Light that we weave with it, joining so many points of Light and creating a new pattern for the world — of Love and consciousness and the merging of the masculine and the feminine."

We decided to begin our journey right away while the tide of this great Love could carry us. We knew that we were placing our lives in God's hands and that our every step was worship. We returned to the Temple of the Women and, of course, my mother had already foreseen this and had packed for us big saddlebags of staples and made a bundle for each of us to carry on our backs. She had arranged for a wagon to carry us well out of Jerusalem. Joseph, my dearest friend, was there as well and had plotted for us our routes that he said had come to him in his hours of prayer and he knew we would be met at every point by those who understood. He also had arranged passage for us to move easily across the Mediterranean on one of his many boats.

We were very grateful. But I knew before we began that we must receive our own guidance. I said to Mary, "We need a place to meditate and make our offering to the living, breathing, most holy One who is ever beyond all names." For you see, even in those days I had difficulty finding words to express the truth of the Creator and I was always reluctant to limit Him/Her through language or through concepts, none of which could hold or describe the limitless Creator.

Mary, although she felt the same, was so deeply focused on the Goddess that it was the expression she always used, and she felt that it was sufficient. But I felt even then that it was easily misunderstood and that the limitations of language allowed divisiveness between human beings to take root and to grow. Even the concept of gender — which is still an issue today — immediately creates that sense of two things, of duality. I must say that the language that I spoke then, the language of Aramaic, was much more conducive to expressing God in all the nuances of Love and beauty. Even so, it felt limiting to me and I struggled with the language and attempted constantly to find a combination of words that would work for all and not be limited. This morning of our departure I had not found it yet.

We spent the rest of the morning and into the afternoon in prayer and meditation in the sweet chapel within the Goddess Temple where we had honored God the previous day. Together our consciousness blended and we saw the pattern of our journey and recognized the gift for humanity in the union that is our Love. God revealed to us in that silence the centers of spirituality that were keeping the spirit alive and functioning in the world. God spoke into my heart and into the heart of my beloved Mary and showed us the great beings who dwelled in each of these points of Light and how these beings of great Godliness, of Light and of Love existed, living directly from the nourishment of the spirit.

We were moved to go, first, to learn from them, and then to allow them to learn from us. The end result would be the weaving of a pattern of Light and beauty, Goddess and God, Divine Masculine and Divine Feminine that would be a heart center for the Earth, a literal *chakra*, an opening to the realms of spirit that would be begun by us, deepened by humanity and brought to life in the Age of Awakening. That Age is now, my friends.

Those who carry the fiat for this awakening of the heart of the world are you. The pattern of our journey was a wheel of Light so luminous, it was almost blinding, even to the inner sight. As it pulsed and throbbed and danced and turned in radiant splendor, we saw together how God moved us. The Creator poured down the Light through me, and drew upwards the nourishment of the Earth, of grounded-ness and beauty through Mary. It was joined in our hearts and our Love-Making, creating that new opening and a continuity of spiritual life that had never before been viable on Earth.

Having taken this time to meditate, I felt much better. I knew, then, that we were beginning our journey with the Creator's blessing. Not only was our itinerary clear but it would always come directly from the spirit. I felt, as Mary did, that it was time to honor our families, our families of friendship, our families of Love and our families of blood. We decided to take the rest of that day and spend it with our dear ones in

Jerusalem and then we would journey the next day to Bethany to tarry a little while with my friends, and especially with Lazarus, for I felt an urgency to see him. The day after we would embark on our journey, every step of which truly wasn't ours but belonged to the Nameless One.

I fall into the undefined depths
of a love that can baptize and cleanse
and heal infinite hearts,
as I nestle into a beauty too vast
to ever abide in a word.

Chapter Twenty

"I felt a velvet darkness... unfathomable... that floated my cells..."

As we left the little chapel within the Goddess Temple, that sacred place that had been so important to us at this time of our wedding, we were full of excited plans for embarking on our journey of exploration, but also excited about being emissaries for God. We walked hand-in-hand into the Temple courtyard, intending to get Mary's belongings and begin our trip to Bethany and beyond.

Of course, we planned on saying farewell to our friends and family but our vision was roaming outward as if it were skipping down the road in front of us, singing. So when we walked into the Temple courtyard, at first I was confused by what I was seeing. All around us people began singing. There were arches of flowers over the walkway. As we walked, flower petals were thrown before our feet and hands reached out in benediction.

I turned to my beloved and raised my eyebrows in an unspoken question. By the look on her face, I could tell that she had her suspicions, though she did seem genuinely surprised. We were herded very lovingly into the largest of the places of worship within the Temple. It was larger than what you would call a chapel, not quite as large as your big churches. As we entered, a great song rose up with hundreds of voices singing from within the chapel of the Temple and outside. The songs were about the unity of God and Goddess and of the opening of a New Age and the coming of balance to the world.

These songs were so uplifting and so filled with timeless harmonies that my heart instantly made its agreement and began to sing with them. Somehow I knew those beautiful voices and I knew those ancient songs. I turned to my beloved, joined hands and kissed her. I said, "You are my Goddess." Together we worshiped in joy. As we stood in the midst of that crowd of people, I began to feel that I was given new eyes to see. When I looked at her, I began to see something deeper, something that whispered to my heart and consciousness — something timeless like the songs that were being sung all around us.

We were pushed lovingly up to the altar and asked to kneel together. The high priestess and priest of the Goddess Temple began anointing us and giving us their blessings as the hands and heart of the God and Goddess in the world. I knew that they truly understood what Mary and I had come to Earth to bring. They were acknowledging us as the incarnation of the living Love in its great splendor as two energies that ever move together.

When we stood and turned and looked out upon the shining faces singing, I saw that they were evenly divided between men and women. They were not separated as they were in the Jewish Temple. They were all standing together, some holding hands, but in exact proportion to each other. I understood more deeply than before why this had been the portal to my marriage with Mary, and with what powerful accord they now beheld us, verifying our mission for the world.

Before I knew it, we were completely caught up in the celebration and found ourselves raising our voices in hymns to the endless movement of the cosmos, of All That Is as it lives and breathes in the vastness and in the world. The songs became prayers, the prayers became dances and the dances brought lightness and joy.

The sacred space was opened then, and there was feasting — and what an amazing feast it was! We laughed, and spoke of the thread of purpose that wove into our lives and joined our spirits. That whole day was spent speaking only of the wonder and the truth of the Creator. It was such food for the spirit, such an upliftment of the soul and such waves of healing for the physical bodies of all those who were present. I saw more deeply than ever how God is our food and drink and how the Creator's Love is our source of nourishment. Only from that can we create our lives wherever we are in all the universes, including here on Earth.

As the sun once again began to set, I could hardly believe the day was ending. It had passed so quickly on gilded wings of community and communion and the movement of spirit and all its blessings. But there was more before us. Mary and I were to be honored once again with the advent of the night as the coming together of the Divine Masculine and Divine Feminine, bringing new life to the world.

A new ritual unfolded. It was completely focused on preparing the energy for us to engage in Divine Love-Making to bring the Creator's Love consciously to Earth. More than ever I was amazed and honored by the level of consciousness of these beautiful people who were so awake. They truly beheld our mission and our purpose together.

All the while through all the celebrations and singing and dancing and through the sacred movements of the evening's ritual, I caught glimpses of my mother and her beloved, Joseph, the one who on Earth was my father. I saw the laughter, so free, the openness on her face, the pure delight in his eyes as Joseph watched her and the sparks when their hands touched. Seeing their closeness being celebrated openly in this swirling dance of loving people touched my heart deeply.

Mary, my mother, had always been the steadfast and shining Light that guided our way in everything. In matters of the spirit, the heart and the family, she had always been at the helm in her quiet and mysterious way. Joseph had ever been there to support her, to ground her, to keep her safe. To see him laughing and to see her pure ecstasy was such a gift to me. When I turned back to look at my beloved and saw the shining Love in her eyes, a prayer rose up from the very depths of my heart within me, thanking God for these blessings and for the gift of this life.

We were escorted to the marriage chamber, the chamber dedicated to just this ritual, the great merging of the Divine Masculine and the Divine Feminine, what became known ultimately as the Great Rite. In those days it was spoken of with wonder and reverence and the true sense of its cosmic power — its deep and moving significance for bringing the life of God in humanity into balance for the refurbishment of the world.

Mary and I entered the wedding chamber and found ourselves in a room that looked as though its walls were adobe. The room was laid out with symbols of the masculine and feminine everywhere. The bed in the center was surrounded with oil lamps and an altar stood at the side. At the head was a painting of the great *Caduceus* upon the golden seal of Solomon which I recognized as the symbol of the merging of the masculine and the feminine, what some would name the *Merkabah* and others see as the Star of David.

It was the symbol of the movement of spirit in that explosion of life that brings forth consciousness and creates all life as the expression of this glorious merging of the masculine and feminine. The *Caduceus*, the two snakes rising along the column of silver light, was also the merging of masculine and feminine as the Double Helix of God. The bed covers were made of silk and other fabrics that were shimmering as white and gold.

Beyond this, all I saw was my beloved, her shining countenance and her amazing eyes and how the light danced off her curls of golden red that swayed when she moved and touched her waist. She turned to me, laughing as always, took my hand and very gently gave me a kiss. At this, there was a great shout from those who had accompanied us. Smiling at each other, they turned and left, placing before the door another symbol of God and Goddess, embraced in this joining.

Thus began our night of conscious Love-Making where every movement was done in service. As we touched and wove our fingers and sank together onto our shining and opulent bed, I could feel myself dissolving until I could touch her very atoms. As I did, I knew just how the atoms sang as a body and that my job was to raise them up and to attune each one to that glorious Light that lives within me every moment and blazes through my heart.

I began this conscious attunement but then to my great surprise, as Mary lay her hand upon my heart, I began to feel a deeper and more powerful energy than I had ever felt from her before. It moved into me, bringing an attunement unlike anything that I had previously experienced. What I felt was a velvet darkness, rich, deep and unfathomable, that drew me down and wrapped around me. It filled my consciousness and floated my cells.

I understood in that timeless moment that this was the sweet wonder of the Creator as the feminine, as the ocean of stillness before the masculine stirred. The Light blazed through me to her. The rich velvet darkness was what she fed me, until together we became a song of Creation moving with the one moment that is ever and always occurring. The darkness became the Light and the Light moved upon the deep and our bodies began to move together. A deep urging rose in me to join our hearts and to recognize what we already were — this great shining center of Love.

As I drew my beloved to me and tasted her lips again and lost myself in her emerald eyes, our breaths became one breath that Love was breathing. Our bodies strained to be together as our very atoms began exchanging their precious energy and acknowledging that eternal flow, the movement of the masculine and the feminine that is the ecstasy of God.

With greatest tenderness we shed our clothing and with reverence our bodies merged. The great Light blazed until it seemed that it would obliterate that darkness and simply shoot us forth into the cosmos. But then, as Mary pulled me even closer in our merging and we lay upon that bed of Light, I lost all bearing and felt that I was purely consciousness moving upon the ocean of Love. Then, as the Goddess, as the great Divine Feminine, Mary reached forth and touched my heart and drew me down into the living pulsing velvet darkness that also was the Earth.

I became a part of the chorus of singing life that wove itself upon that darkness and created the most beautiful patterns of colors, colors that became the life of the Earth. Suddenly I recognized what she had been showing me in this movement beyond words — that in the Earth was held the keys to all the treasures of God. All that had been lost to humanity was held in trust, wrapped in the velvet protected soil of the Earth's darkness — that incarnation of the feminine as the world. I understood with my heart's perception that in our merging she was given the expansiveness that was my reality and I was gifted with the rich and timeless depth of life in which she lived.

I had thought that I knew everything, or my heart did, about the magnificent movements of our Creator and the patterns and illusions that became life in the world. But I never knew the rich and velvet ocean of that attunement with the Creator's Love that is the feminine until that night. I also had not understood that the pearl of the world is humanity's treasure chest, that special vault in which you have stored all of your treasures. Every key to every secret in the living cosmos is held in sacred trust for you there, wrapped in the soil, held in the movements of Nature and the patterns of her voice. It speaks through every color, each season, every landscape in all the world, creating a tapestry of holy awakening the moment the key is remembered.

The key to it all is the divine Love-Making, the true union of the masculine and feminine that opens the way to all of the treasures that you have stored for yourselves, the garden of God's perfection waiting to be restored. In those moments I became that treasure and I found the elixir of the life of the living Creator just as present in that rich tapestry in the world of Nature as I had ever found in the living cosmos.

As we became that glorious and endless ecstasy together, that grand explosion of orgasmic joy far beyond the simple responses of a physical body, I was awed. I was amazed and I was reverent. It was the joining of the two grand forces of life in a great crescendo of holy worship and joy. In that joining, in that moment of climactic wonder, the two became truly one and we extended from the depths of the Earth and its wonders all the way into the glorious vastness. We reached the pinnacle of Light and explosive Love that is Creation in its ongoing explosion of ecstasy.

If you go within, you will find this truth of Love within your hearts because each of you is ever and always participating in this great movement of the universe that is the joining of the masculine and feminine, two parts of your greater being. That which you call your Twin Flame's Love is the reflection of the Creator before you in every dimension of reality in the living moment, and it is never ending. The key, of course, is your heart and the heart's true remembrance of the wholeness of your being and the Creator's Love. That Love shows you your heart as the power of Love beating — the masculine and feminine ever joining into that great explosion of orgasmic ecstasy that is conscious life.

What Mary and I planted that night in the Temple was the awakening of this life in its fullness with all of its treasures and all of its cosmic movement regained for humanity. I could see the many layers of time and the centuries that would pass until that seed that we planted would come to fruition — the turning of a whole Age. That time is here.

When we awakened in the night it was for the joining to happen all over again. We Made Love with passion and with tenderness, but always with humanity in our hearts. The spirit of the living God spoke to me and said once again, "It has begun." I saw the weaving that was Mary and I together creating for humanity that bridge, that return to full conscious awareness of the presence of all of the treasures of God and the acceptance once again of the Creator's Love fully awakened in humankind. Between the great movements of the cosmos that shattered our consciousness and sent us shimmering through the stars, we came back to Earth and sat before the altar in prayer together, praying to be the clear conduit for this pure and amazing Love to be revealed once again to the world.

Through all those hours of revelation and joy, that night I was shown that while I could embrace the whole of life and hold the vibration of truth and the center steadily with Mary, I could not do this for humankind. I could hold it as the Christos but that humankind must make its own agreement. Humanity must regain the treasures that it had buried, and once again choose to open the heart and restore balance.

The voice of the spirit said to me as I looked into the eyes of my beloved, "They cannot do it without you, My beloved Jeshua and your beloved Mary. You must build the bridge back to Me for them, for they have forgotten the way. Right now they cannot even make this decision. You turn the key in the lock to regain possession of their hearts because the chasm of the choice for separation is too wide."

I understood that it was my choice to make a sacrifice that would cross that chasm and build that bridge. As I looked in Mary's eyes I saw that she was also receiving this and that we understood our commitment. What she had given me this night in that velvet darkness, in that understanding of the Earth and the treasures held within it, was her power to create this miracle with me. She would hold the pattern of life embodied in the world as the Divine Feminine so clearly that I could use it as the anchor from which I could stretch for humanity across that chasm.

I knew the Creator and the great Light of the cosmic presence. I knew that I could reach that. But whether I could bring humanity with me was the question. The rootedness that Mary gave me, her gift to me was the presence of the feminine and its joy and effervescence that always lived within her. This was the essence of life that would allow her to hold the pattern of energy that we are as the heart of the Christos and anchor it in the world. We would then be able to align with the voice of Nature, and bringing all of those patterns to bear, cross the chasm of separation from the Creator to bring humanity all the way Home.

The voice of God within me kept assuring me of my success. I really must say, of our success, for even then, I knew that without my beloved it would be impossible. I could not hold the pattern for humanity well enough, clearly enough while stretching into that pure communion, without that anchoring Love that she so fully offered me.

As I looked at Mary and she looked at me, and as we touched and joined and loved and prayed and dedicated our lives to serving humanity — all that we saw was the Creator's perfect Love. What we heard was God's singing voice between us, and we felt that Love pouring into us and bringing us that perfect Light. Our joy rose up in ecstatic worship. Our hearts sang that eternal "Yes" that is the opening that brings the acceptance of pure life energy and the great Love that is ever and always waiting for us as the gift from our beloved God.

We spent three days in the Temple celebrating, feasting, sharing in community and spending our nights making Sacred Love ever more consciously. As she took me into that velvet darkness again, I felt the endless ocean of the Creator's Love as the feminine. As I reached into the Earth, I also felt the refraction of the Light — that pure Light that is the Divine Masculine. I could see how the masculine aspect of the Creator's Love was being distorted by humanity and how the

Goddess would spend the next 2000 years searching for him.

With my beloved Mary I planted the seed that would bring back the true and holy union that is the perfect balance of Divine Masculine and Divine Feminine in the world. The moments that you are living now are the doorway to this. They are the point in the wheel of time for the fruition of those seeds that Mary and I planted together in those nights in the Temple.

the miracle that we exist at all
sings out from every star
turning and turning and
turning in the arms
of the spiraling
light of
love

Chapter Twentyone

"What we understood in the depths of our hearts was a service to Love unimaginable."

I opened my eyes on the morning of the fourth day after our arrival at the Goddess Temple. My heart was filled with elation, a joy that I felt nothing could contain. I heard the sound of life around me, the sound of sandaled feet upon the walkway, the sounds of many voices embracing the day and weaving together a sense of community.

I reached instantly for my beloved's hand and turned her toward me that I might gaze upon her beautiful face. That face to me totally contained the unspeakable beauty of the living Goddess. I found myself in awe at the wonder and the power of my feelings for her and the depth of my connection to the movement of Love that is the essence of our Creator.

When she stretched and opened her eyes and I saw that emerald green gazing at me, all I could do was smile and put her hand upon my heart. I was overwhelmed by the depth of these feelings and the magnitude of what moves between us, and my bemusement shown upon my face.

Even though I felt that we had flown through the magnificent cosmos and danced in spirit with the stars, at this moment I could feel a profound sense of impending revelation that held a portent that I could not fathom. As I felt this movement of spirit, mixed with the wonder of this Love, there was a call deep within me with which I was totally familiar. It was the call to silence, to witnessing the vastness, to making myself available once again to the living voice of God.

As Mary touched my cheek and softly kissed my lips, a wordless communication passed between us and I knew that she was sensing the same thing. It was a while before I could speak. Then I took both of her hands in mine and said, "My beautiful Mary, I believe our plans are changing. You know I was intending to go with you today to Bethany and to prepare there to embark upon our journey — that journey that we've been called to as the witnesses for Love, in service to the living holy God."

She laughed at my seriousness which was always her way and said, "Of course, Jeshua. We must live by that voice, by the movement of the living spirit within. I know that we cannot plan. We cannot plan with our minds — not anything. We must be ready to go where the Goddess sends us and to listen to Her voice guiding us in every moment. I am thrilled to accept this guidance and to live this life with you. I give my will this day, completely, to Her. I embark with joy into what this day brings."

Sharing a passionate kiss, we rose and made ready to make our way out of the Temple and into the desert where I felt strongly we were called to spend time in the silence and the spaciousness and to let the spirit speak in new ways. We had allowed that living spirit to ignite us in passion and to move us in a grand

and glorious dance together, sharing the joy of our union with this community of men and women. We had honored the movement of God and Goddess embodied within us.

But this was something different. I could feel it to my depths and I sensed that it would bring to me a far deeper understanding of what we had come to do. So we made our rounds and said farewell to all those precious hearts and faces until we came to the room where my mother and father were staying — my mother and father of the Earthly realm.

I held my mother tightly and relished her essence. I breathed in her scent, took in her Love and marveled at her beauty and her soft yet strong dedication to holding the highest Light and holding the vision of God for humanity and for the awakening of Love.

Then I held Joseph's hand and looked upon his beloved face. I noticed that his face was looking older and I smiled at him and poured forth My Love. I said the words but knew they couldn't hold it, couldn't express the depth of my gratitude to them. Mary truly honored them with the things she said and felt. There was a harmony, a true accord among us and a shared vision and purpose.

We went then to also say goodbye to Mary's mother. It was poignant. I could feel that there was a new level of Love and forgiveness. Our Love — my Love with Mary, the Magdalene — had brought a renewal, had washed her heart of the old pain and the perceived wounds of abandonment that my Mary had felt being a daughter of the Temple and not of her mother.

I could see a pattern emerging of the healing of their Love and I said a prayer of gratitude in my heart as I whispered, "Thank You, beloved God, holy, omnipotent One, the living, breathing Alpha and Omega. Thank You for this blessing. Let these blessings now be multiplied. Let Love grow between them and let it grow in every heart in the world."

And so we left the Temple of the Goddess. We left the song of the women and we left the courtyard, the Temple that had nurtured us and acknowledged the importance of our Love for each other and our marriage. We walked out into the desert from Jerusalem, a walk that took us most of the day. There was a plateau, a mesa, a hill made of ancient rock that rose up out of the vast and open scenery of the desert. In this hill were a number of caves. I drew Mary into one of them.

Without needing to speak a word, we settled down to meditate, each of us giving ourselves over to the experience and opening to whatever the Creator had for us. We released our perceptions of time and our little wills and itineraries. Breathing deeply we reached out and held hands and slipped into the Light.

That evening was simply a falling away of the world of experience. I could feel the Light washing away the layers of reason and understanding and perception of the mind. Even though these did not hold me as they did humanity, I could see how much I used these things to communicate with people and how they took even me away from that ecstatic union. As we rose into the pure Light, I felt Mary's spirit with me perfectly as we became two blazing flames, worshiping God. Our hearts cried out in our deep and powerful worship and that movement within us that said, "God, You are my everything."

In the spirit we opened ourselves to the living One completely. With heart and soul and being we said, "God, Creator, use me. Let Your Will, Your Love live through me." When our meditation was done, we went outside into the gathering dusk and found some gnarled pieces of old dried wood given to us as a gift by the twisted and bent trees that grew few and far between on this hill. We created a small fire and sat beneath the endless sky, watching together as the stars made their appearance.

That endless sky was so beautiful and it spoke to us of eternity and of all the Beings of Light who light the heavens. We spoke not a single word because words were not needed. We were in such accord that we were one consciousness and one heart. All that I felt, she felt. All that I knew, she was also knowing. The living breath of the spirit moved between us and whispered our instructions.

That night we made our bed with the cloaks we had brought with us. We lay at the mouth of the cave upon the hard ground together. Heart-to-heart we looked into each other's eyes and joined, first *chakra* to *chakra*, then, etheric bodies, and then, our very energies merged. Rather than going to sleep, we moved out into greater consciousness and let our bodies rest, while we explored.

In that way we spent our night, traveling together, connected to humanity around the world, also allowing the Masters of Light to show us all that was needed to make the way for the bridging that was to be our life's work. We saw all the ways that humankind had turned its energy upon itself and developed a way of living that was selfishness, based on a law that was the reversal of God's Love. It was the law of taking for oneself, "looking out for number one," as you would say.

We saw how the energies of Light had become congested and then become frozen as they continued to turn in a vortex moving inward on itself. It created what looked like a great tornado, a funnel cloud of "anti-Love" that left a huge void into which the hearts of humanity had fallen.

While we watched and learned and understood, we saw the world of ego — that false construct that lives by this reversal and divides the world into a duality of experience rather than the truth of Love that is the only thing that is real. As we watched and learned and saw the patterns of energy, we also experienced our Love alive and blazing. We began to comprehend that our Love had the power to warm these hearts, to unwind this reversal of Love — to melt what had been frozen, to bring the barrenness that had become the inner landscape of humankind back to life. This is a landscape that many of you know intimately, a landscape of fear, and all the ways it shows itself in the symbols of an Earthly life — lack, scarcity, anguish, loneliness, depravity and always the focus on the little self, the personality.

This was a time of learning for me. Until this, I had lived my life constantly and simply bathed in the endless joy and wonder of a world of beauty and harmony and joy. The Angels spoke. The birds sang with God's voice. All of Nature accorded the perfection of the living holographic harmony in which the One that lives in me lives in everyone. This is the world that is to be returned at last to humanity in this time of change that focuses on you. Until that time, I had been an innocent in the ways of the world, and truly I still was, though I didn't think so. All the things I had learned in the desert silence that night made me feel that I had become a man of greater wisdom.

When morning came, we rose together and broke our fast on goat cheese and olives, I felt another movement of great importance. Mary looked at me and without a word needing to be said, we joined hands and walked up the side of the hill, scrambling over rocks and around the gnarled trees that stuck out from the side. We reached the top, the plateau, which gave us an open vision of the desert. We sat down together immediately and began to pray and to meditate — to open ourselves to whatever was knocking on the door of our hearts. We waited.

After probably an hour there was a great shower of Light. Then there came a huge wave of sadness and an amazing presence came before us in agony. It said, "My name is Lucifer and I am here to ask your help and to tell you my story." I knew this being! With a jolt I remembered this glorious Archangel of magnificent Light who had spoken across the Heavens and always worshiped God, and who, with his Divine Counterpart, had been one of the greatest Lights. I remembered honoring him and praying to be such a Light, unwavering always in my service to the Nameless One.

My breath caught when I recognized the deep sense of pain within him. I asked him in my heart, "Lucifer, what is it? I know you and I know your Light."

I looked at Mary briefly and I understood she was with me. All that I was seeing, she was seeing too. She squeezed my hand and I saw a tear rolling down her cheek. I knew that my beloved felt his pain. The sense of his counterpart, the feminine Archangel, I was so weak, so distant we could hardly feel her.

I opened my heart and prayed and said, "God, give us the Light. Pour Your Love through us that You might be his strength. Bless this Archangel who has always worshiped You and let us be the instrument for relieving him of whatever this suffering is." Then Lucifer revealed to us his service to the Creator. As he spoke into our hearts, God supported him and verified every concept, verified each word, although what he showed us was instant and beyond mortal thought. What we understood in the depths of our hearts was a service to Love unimaginable.

Lucifer had given himself to humanity in a sacrifice of selflessness and such deep service that he became one with the human energy. He agreed to be the consciousness that created for humankind a wall of protection within which humanity could live and play out the decision to believe that they were separate from God. His body of Light became the membrane that is the etheric body of the Earth in which the experience of duality, of the thoughts of good and evil could play out all probabilities, all possibilities of living separate from God.

We deeply felt how it had affected him. That which had been such a glorious freedom of Light, of being, one who was free to move through the living cosmos, had become so dense in vibration, so wrapped up in the reversal of energy and the pain of humanity that he had become frozen, physical. He had become the consciousness of the world of duality. Every moment that he lived this, he yet remembered the truth of his passionate Love for the Light that never wavered and the universe that holds no opposites.

In the remembering of freedom was his torture because he had taken on the consciousness that became the world of men and women, and thus, he had forgotten so much of himself that he had almost lost contact with his Twin Flame, his Divine Counterpart, the balance for his masculine being. All of this we understood in an instant.

I fell to my face on the hilltop and I cried out as I felt his pain. I cried to the Heavens and to the God that lives within me. I said, "Oh God, the living Alpha and Omega, our Father and Mother, I ask that you release him." The Creator's voice said to me, "And so it shall be done through you, Jeshua, and your beloved Mary. This is what you are here to do. You are here to lift this mantle of oppression, not only from Lucifer but from every human being. You are here to restore the truth, to make the consciousness that there is only Love accessible once again to humankind. It shall be done through you."

As I looked and felt and understood in the depths of my being and in my heart what it meant that this world lived a reality far different from the reality I had traveled thus far, I understood more clearly what was coming. I understood what it was I had to do to accomplish this bridge and to bring back the truth to humankind. I knew that I would have to live deeply and profoundly the experience that now held Lucifer.

I would have to acknowledge it, accord it, connect to it and bring it back to the truth of the One. I would bring back the truth of Love and only Love as the truth of all Creation — the endless Love of God I AM that lives in every human heart and shows itself in every aspect of Nature. But as I sat on that plateau that day in the desert I had no idea how I would accomplish this. I only knew it was my destiny. We, together, Mary and I, had seen patterns. We had intuited what would occur but we still didn't know any particulars. We simply knew we had to live in trust.

In this trust in our Creator, we both pledged that day that we would free our beloved Lucifer from the confines of his prison, the prison that was his by choice and by the choices of humankind. Even then I grasped that I didn't understand either the depths of his pain or the breadth of his service. Nor did I understand how to bring him back to his beloved, to the great Twin Flame Love that was his destiny, his truth. I now knew this truth as what I shared with my Mary and had come to see it is the truth of every person. I had seen how the Creator had made every heart.

I lay there, my spirit filled with Lucifer's pain, my eyes filled with tears. Mary laid her head across my back and held me. We both deeply felt Lucifer in our hearts. Again, I said from the depths of my heart and being, "God, I vow to free him and I ask You to help me. I do this together with my beloved. Let Mary and me be this bridge! Beloved Creator of All That Is, live here as us and show us exactly what to do in the living moment, constantly." I received that deep "Yes" within my being. I knew my prayers were answered. I felt God's great Love as it moved throughout my energy field. I felt the change in the atmosphere that was the answer to that prayer.

I saw in that larger vision that I would have another meeting with Lucifer in this same place in the desert and that the meeting would be totally misunderstood. But its truth would be based on this foundation of friendship, and mutual service to the living God.

I was shaken by this encounter. When I sat up afterwards, I couldn't move. I just cleared my mind of all thought and opened my heart so that God could use it and I embraced the silence. There was nothing else right then that I could do. I knew that at that moment it was beyond me to understand how to reweave that pattern and to make Lucifer's service a success, for at that moment it didn't look like one. It looked like failure — as though all that he had hoped had come to naught.

He had believed his Love for God, his Light, could free humanity and give them back what they had lost. He had believed that he could raise up the energy and by his own Love unfreeze the hearts that already were frozen and remake the density that was the cooling of human energies, based upon the decision to believe in other than only Love. He discovered that he couldn't do this, for humanity has free will. And yet, I felt the call of God within me and I knew that God, our Father and Mother, was coming for humanity's hearts. I knew also that Mary and I were to be an instrument in this awakening of the world.

Thus began my meetings with Lucifer of which there were many but three important ones that set the course of my service and clarified my mission for the world. These prepared us for that which was to come, most of which you already know, but which I didn't know clearly at that time. However, I had intuited the gist of it and I had read the signs in the Heavens.

I did understand the energies that had been practiced since the beginning of time when one who comes to be the living sacrifice takes on the darkness and the distance from God and brings it back to the Light. Almost every culture before that time had experience or acknowledgement of this, at least in their rituals. But until my life, such things had been limited to certain beings coming to serve a certain people.

I was here to serve all of humankind and to somehow be a living bridge back to Love. So it was that the unfolding of our work began in deeper and deeper ways as we came to understand the movements of Creation and to be the embodiment of the Light. Now we had come to see another portent and to find the recognition of this great being, Lucifer. My life was filled with many such communions, with the Masters, with the Angels, with the energies of Nature, but rarely had something impacted me like this. Until this time I had lived my life above the human vibration.

I had lived the vibration of the pure Light of the living God and it had appeared before me as the world. I had studied and come to know deeply the Torah, and I had studied almost every religion. I had understood concepts of duality and the separation from the Creator's Love that was felt by the majority of human beings. But it wasn't real to me until I met

Lucifer. He was the embodiment of that pain — of being separate from the Creator's Love until the energy became so slow, so dense that the physical world of frozen Love ensued.

Having known him in his glory as a pure and shining Light for God and finding him now so limited, distressed and calcified moved me, shook me and opened me to the plight of humankind. I became a fervent prayer to serve the glorious Love of God, the I AM, and to bring to humanity the Love I knew, heart and soul and mind, the Love that lived and sang within me all the time. I became the dedication to give humanity this — to bring this Love I had found with Mary, my beloved Magdalene, that blazed through the Heavens and found the ecstasy of Creation, and to return the gifts of God to humankind, immediately if I could.

Mary in her wisdom, smiled at me and took my hands in hers. She said, "Jeshua, you must breathe. Let's take a break from feeling the importance of our mission and just take time to celebrate our Love." She lifted me back up just like the butterfly rises from the chrysalis into the sunlight. In her Love I rose again into that living joy that was our every moment together. As she smoothed my hair and rubbed the tears from my cheek, she said, "She will guide us in every step. The Creator knows what we must do to bridge this pain, and you know that we will do it.

"So right now let us live in this moment and let us be these passionate hearts, that we might join in Love on every possible level — from that glorious explosion of Light and Love to this, that which we experience in bodies." And so it was that I regained my perspective and returned to the joy in which I always lived. That which I understood from that meeting with Lucifer — while it lived in me and was a constant — never again took me into the depths of despair as it had that morning.

From that point on, our time became serenity, as we simply sat and felt the Light and drank the Love. I led Mary into the experience that I often had of becoming a great star of pure Light. As she joined me in this experience of the living Light of God, as we merged in that unity, I became the blazing white and she became a magnificent star of gold. Our rays merged and danced and joined, gold and white together, and we became the luminous movement of Love throughout Creation, the joining of the two energies that are the movement of Creation itself.

We passed two more days in the desert quiet, communing with the sky and stars, with the vast intelligence that is Nature, as we spoke with the wind and prayed to the Deva of air and took joy in the gift of the Earth. At night we would light a fire and salute the spirit of fire and how it manifested as the explosion of God, bringing Light and warmth into the world.

Our time passed and the harmony between us grew until we rarely spoke at all but rather thought our thoughts into each other's consciousness and we breathed — truly — the same breath. We also found ourselves in communication, effortlessly, with my mother and Joseph. At times, we felt the connection with the Temple of Women. I also found myself aware of the Essenes. We began to find that we were part of a greater community of beings who were all in communion in the spirit.

When the time came for us to leave the desert, we bundled up our cloaks and our few provisions, put our sandals on our feet and embarked, turning our face toward Bethany. We felt joy in our hearts. We held a shared connection to the beauty of the natural world and to the strata of energy that you would call Eden — that energy of life that was meant for humanity and that humanity enjoyed until the choice for separation became the foremost choice in the minds and hearts of men and women, and the world changed.

As I walked out of the desert that morning holding my beloved's hand in mine, soft, white, delicate, with her red gold hair brushing across my arms, I knew that we had deepened our spiritual maturity. I also could feel the truth of two worlds interwoven together but whose energies were not the same at all.

There was the world that I had lived in from the time I was born. This was a world in which my communion with the Creator was constant, in which the grasses and the flowers would bow their heads to me when I walked and the night sky would speak of the movements of Ages. I would see the Angels' Light bathing me at night. All around me was always beauty. I was continually surrounded by the faces of those I loved who carried their own deep and beautiful wisdom, provided by the unending movement of the Creator's limitless Love.

Then, there was the world in which lived most of humanity that I began to see more clearly. This world was based on the separation from the Father/Mother's Love and thus was filled with fear. It was totally foreign to me and I could hardly begin to comprehend it. Yet, my encounter with Lucifer had made it real to me and made me understand that part of my mission was to release this needless suffering and to bring the God's Love back to humanity in all its fullness.

With a sense of growing awareness of the purpose before me and the power of this Love I shared with Mary, my heart was full with the overflowing joy of serving the God I love, heart and soul. Thus we began our walk to Bethany and to the next phase of our journey.

This is the first in a coming series of books in which Jeshua and Mary are revealing, through Yael and Doug Powell, the previously untold story of their life on Earth. Volume II, **Jesus and Mary Magdalene: Creating the Pattern of Light for Earth,** brings us the next segment of their lives and their fascinating travels to different parts of our planet. It will be available later this year.

If you have enjoyed this book and would like to be informed through our mailing list of future books, please email us at connect@circleoflight.net.

About Yael and Doug Powell
And Circle of Light

Yael Powell began meditating as part of her ministerial training many years ago. For over forty years she has had a daily communion with God that she has faithfully recorded. She stands in the tradition of Hildegard von Bingen and other mystics who found God's loving voice through experiences of great suffering transformed into Love.

In 1983 Yael was diagnosed with a painful progressive disease of the spine. She was in excruciating physical and emotional pain, a true dark night of the soul that ended the active life she had known. In her darkest moment, she called out to God for help. "Suddenly I began to be lifted to a place of great beauty, of sparkling light, and I was filled with an amazing energy that felt like dancing golden rain. I felt the loving presence of God." Each day Yael began to receive beautiful visions during meditation which gave her strength and the courage to live in her painful physical condition. She faithfully recorded these experiences with her words, becoming "the pen in God's hand." These Messages continue to this day and fill over 100 spiral bound notebooks and a large number of tapes.

In 1986 after her marriage to Doug Powell, the God Messages intensified and began unfolding the SoulMate teaching, new to the planet, and their path of service as SoulMates. The Messages helped Yael and Doug grow through Yael's release of a childhood of incest and pain, the loss of a child and through the challenges that disability can bring to a marriage. They grew as a couple from ego-relating to a heart-centered relationship.

In 1999 Yael and Doug moved from the center of Eureka Springs (AR) out to "the lake" and under God's direction, formed their spiritual center, Circle of Light, in a magnificent setting. They are ministers in their own wedding chapel and share the Messages from God and their experiences through workshops and the Say "Yes" to Love series of books (Circle of Light Press), as well as through CD's, DVD's and their websites.

Yael has the gift of being a "universal communicator" and often takes Messages from Jesus and Mother Mary as well as from our Creator. In autumn of 2008, Jeshua spontaneously began giving the story of his life on Earth through Yael during her meditation time. Soon it became apparent that this was to be a series of books, telling the truth of that powerful incarnation in a way it had never before been told. This book is the first of that series.

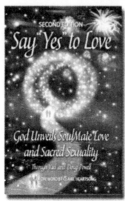

CIRCLE OF LIGHT ORDER FORM
SAY 'YES' TO LOVE SERIES

Please send the following:

____ copies of *Jesus and Mary Magdalene, The Eternal Heart of Love, Volume I* @ $22.95 ($5 S&H) _____

____ copies of *God Explains Soulmates* @ $11 ($5 S&H) _____

____ copies of *God Unveils SoulMate Love & Sacred Sexuality* @ $20.00 ($5 S&H)

____ copies of *Eternal Twin Flame Love, The Story of ShannaPra* @ $16 ($5 S&H) _____

____ copies of *God Leads Humanity Toward Christ Consciousness* @ $16 ($5 S&H) _____

____ copies of *Giving Birth to a World of Love* @ $16 ($5 S&H) _____

____ copies of *Magic Cat Explains Creation!* @ $16 ($5 S&H) _____

Prices are for the USA. For postage to other countries, please email us first and we will find the best shipping cost: connect@circleoflight.net

Name: _____

Address: _____

City: _____ State: _____ Zip Code: _____

To use credit cards, please go to our web site OR you may fax your order with credit card to (479) 253-2880.

Name on Card: _____

CC#: _____ Exp. Date: _____

If you would like to be on our email list and receive bi-monthly Messages from God, please fill out the following:

Email address_____

Circle of Light
3969 Mundell Road
Eureka Springs, Arkansas 72631
1-866-629-9894 Toll Free or 479-253-6832 or 2774